ALONE IN AMERICA

ALONE IN AMERICA

THE STORIES THAT MATTER

ROBERT A. FERGUSON

HARVARD UNIVERSITY PRESS

Cambridge, Massachusetts, and London, England

2013

Printed in the United States of America

Library of Congress Cataloging-in-Publication Data
Ferguson, Robert A., 1942–
Alone in America : the stories that matter / Robert A. Ferguson.
p.   cm.
Includes bibliographical references and index.
ISBN 978-0-674-06676-2 (cloth; alk. paper)
1. American fiction—History and criticism.   2. Loneliness in
literature.   I. Title.
PS374.L56F47 2013
813.009'353—dc23   2012027363

For

DCD, DFB, and JMM,

who were there when being alone had its dangers,

and for

Priscilla Parkhurst Ferguson

CONTENTS

ACKNOWLEDGMENTS

John Paul Russo was an important catalyst at every stage of this book. A lifetime of intellectual exchange has made him a touchstone in what I write. Kenji Yoshino read an entire version of the manuscript, gave crucial direction, and offered the kind of advice you only get from a trusted resource, the friend who is also a wise man. Michael T. Gilmore supplied a vital critique of Chapter 2 and knew how to offer support when progress was slow.

My editor, John Kulka, helped me to clarify the larger themes and the organizational structure of the manuscript. His faith in the project and his careful suggestions, never forced, were crucial throughout a period of clarification, revision, and rearrangement. Two anonymous outside evaluators for Harvard University Press made suggestions that strengthened the manuscript in important ways. Gabriel Soto expertly prepared many versions of this work without once asking when was I going to get it right.

Priscilla Parkhurst Ferguson and I have long shared the same study, often across the same table. It is impossible to say how much she has given to this book on a daily basis, from the mundane needs of grammar to the most profound corrections of thought. Nothing helps more than reading aloud to someone who loves you enough to criticize a passage thought perfect. If my expertise is suspect on the subject of isolation, it is because she has been there encouraging and ready to help.

Three festive occasions provided inspiration. In the first, Richard Fulmer helped me see an issue over Sunday brunch. In the second, a glorious wedding banquet, Cathy Sharkey and Ina Bort made suggestions that changed the manuscript. In the third, this time amidst diners in a fine restaurant, John and Lois Widdemer came up with new language. These events were important in another way. Loneliness, it seems, is easier to talk about in happy group settings. It also helps to eat well in good company.

Themes presented in Chapter 1 were discussed in different form as "Rip Van Winkle and Generational Divides in American Culture," *Early American Literature* 40 (Fall 2005): 529–544. Minor aspects of Chapter 6 were developed in another guise in "Immigrant Plight / Immigration Law: A Study in Intractability," *Columbia Journal of Race and Law* 2 (Fall 2012).

ALONE IN AMERICA

Our unhappiness comes from a single thing,

not knowing how to be comfortably alone in a room.

—BLAISE PASCAL, *PENSÉES*

PROLOGUE: THE LORDS OF LIFE

When we say, "I am alone," we mean different things. The phrase is descriptive: we are by ourselves, and yet the words when used have an emotional trajectory. They imply *loneliness* (a negative state), *vulnerability* (a limitation), or *solitude* (a sought condition). The three possibilities are even interchangeable, but each suggests a different understanding of the self and its use of time and space.

Being alone is also a force in America today. More people live by themselves than at any other time in the history of the United States. One out of four households has become single occupancy. One out of four inhabitants has no confidant. One out of four people in the United States admits to loneliness. Many Americans who live together now will also end up alone. So prevalent is the unhappiness of those who find themselves alone that critics have made it a defining trait of modern life, yet no one talks about it except in books. Books, mostly novels, thus become the source of what we will not meet or discuss in any other way.

How is it that an imagined reality can surpass reality itself? We turn to fiction to recognize something in our own lives and the world around us, and no one reads for very long without learning that solitude is an obsession in American literature. The isolated characters in American fiction appeal to us through their inward claims of identity when pitted against the pressures of a surrounding community. They appeal because they indicate how we might talk to ourselves when the pressures come our way.

Religious philosophers describe the way we talk to ourselves as a mysterious inner voice. Secular critics speak of internal conversations that are hard to locate even when they shape what we say we care about. Either way, there is a mysterious side to reflection that is difficult to explain. Fiction answers that difficulty by offering a proving ground for the uses and even the dangers of this internal conversation.

To hear a created character ruminate is to listen to a voice in crisis. We watch an examined life at work, and we want to know how the character's explanations hold up when challenged. The best fiction includes the search for a reliable voice, one that might unlock our own when in crisis or conflict.

Alone in America looks to the moments when experience has turned a speaker inward. We all prefer to be alone at times, but what if we are forced away from others or undone by them, as happens in every life? These are the moments when the space between loneliness and solitude disappears, a situation we welcome only in the realm of story. Fiction, in this sense, is always about a comeuppance endured. We learn to care about characters through their struggle to overcome the world rising against them.

In "Experience," an essay from 1844, Ralph Waldo Emerson called such moments of comeuppance "the lords of life." They represent the times and circumstances in life that cut across everything we want to do or become. Mysterious but suddenly visible, they interrupt and challenge us to the point where we must stop and ask, as Emerson does, "Where do we find ourselves?" *Alone in America* explores these moments through the writers that Americans read most and through characters we cannot forget.

Unavoidable adversaries somewhere in our path, the lords of life appear here in the order of their power over us and in stories that define and overcome them in some way. Success never comes easily in these struggles, and it is achieved only when the lords of life are reduced to manageable linguistic form. Their names in the chapters that follow are *failure, betrayal, change, defeat, breakdown, fear, difference, age,* and *loss.* The felt quality in existence lies in meeting them on their own terms.

Of course, the lords of life disrupt the human condition everywhere, but their disruptions isolate victims in America with a peculiar intensity. As early as 1835, Alexis de Tocqueville identifies a rampant individualism at work that "disposes each member of the community to sever himself from the mass of his fellows and to draw apart with his family and friends," and when each member "has thus formed a little circle of his own," the problems outside of that circle have little meaning until the lords of life decide to enter it. Decline and misfortune have no moral status unless they happen to be your own.

Tocqueville sees many Americans who feel alone in the "Individualism in Democratic Countries" section of *Democracy in America,* and he traces the propensity to the openness, mobility, uncertainty, and flux in a spacious new country, but he is also too acute not to find more intimate causes. A separating individualism thrives on leveling tendencies, distrust of authority, suspicion of others, narrow social engagement, and a presentism that loses interest in relationships across time.

The number of presumed causes for feeling alone tells us something else. Tocqueville comes to regard the vast majority of Americans as *permanently* separated from themselves and with untold consequences. More is involved than "the habit of always considering themselves as standing alone." "Those who went before are soon forgotten, of those who will come after no one has any idea: the interest of [the American] man is confined to those in close propinquity to himself."

Not surprisingly Americans offer their own positive justifications for standing alone. By the late 1830s, the best in America become excited when they are told they must listen to a higher self as their only guide and glory in solitude as their natural state against the trifling norms and conventions of society. Individualism thus becomes the answer as well as the problem to feeling alone, and it soon translates into a series of fables about the solitary adventurer and its social variant, the self-made man.

The strength in this response depends on aspirations in answer to anxieties. Celebrated figures, icons of individualism, have enthralled each generation of Americans down to our own in story, song, and myth, and they remain touchstones for the foreseeable future against all probability and common sense. For no matter how many assertions of self-reliance one finds in the ideology of American individualism, everyone needs companionship, and no one at any level is ever self-made.

The single greatest attribute of American individualism has been this tenacious hold on the nation despite its contradictions and loss of the philosophical underpinnings that gave it birth. Tocqueville described a phenomenon. Ralph Waldo Emerson in "The Divinity School Address" (1838) and "Self-Reliance" (1841) turned the phenomenon into an ideological boast: "That is always best which gives me to myself"; "Let me admonish you, first of all, to go alone, to refuse the good models, even those most sacred to the imagination of men"; "Absolve you to yourself. Nothing is at last sacred but the integrity of your own mind."

Behind the boasts of self-reliance are philosophical premises justifying the claim, but they have not worn well. Emerson and other romantic idealists assume a solitary "aboriginal self" in control of an innate moral sense based on "God within." This self enjoys an unmediated relation with the universe through the benevolence of nature, and its mental adventures into the wholeness of things exceed anything society has to offer. Human history is thus not an account of civilizations so much as the story of individuals who have made a difference and who realize that the puzzles, connections, and complexities in life resolve themselves into a discoverable unity with the infinite one.

Some of the country's greatest literature comes from debate over these transcendentalist premises, and yet every one of them has been challenged and dismissed by later forms of accepted understanding. Pragmatism posits a pluralistic universe in which only experimentation can counter the ambiguity in consequences. Behaviorism and sociology reject the possibility of an innate moral sense. Modern psychology denies a unified self. Astronomy has discovered an immense inanimate universe with no apparent interest in humankind. Darwinism sets aside the benevolence of nature. More empirical conceptions of history have undermined the great-man theory of history.

Nonetheless, and against every intellectual onslaught, American individualism continues to flourish. The desire for, and assertion, and expectation of self-reliance remain national values, even though they are far more difficult to explain and sustain without the support of a philosophical comfort zone. It is, after all, harder to stand alone if the cosmos does not care about you. The pleasures in nature continue, but few contemporary Americans regard them as a conduit of divine will. Anyone now alone must cope with a very different understanding of the self to reach a solitude worthy of the name.

It is again Alexis de Tocqueville who gives us our first glimpse of the strongest support that remains. When the author of *Democracy in America* claims that the American citizen lives "confined to those in close propinquity to himself," he glimpses the All-American family, or what is known today as "family values." If that phrase has become controversial, a simpler synonym has not: "home." Even Emerson, who denigrates the closest familial connections in his stress on self-reliance, argues "the wise man stays at home." "Home is where the heart is": this popular American adage lifted from the Roman philosopher Pliny the Elder conveys a significance that the word "house" cannot. To lose one's home conveys a level of devastation far beyond loss of a place.

The most influential American theologian of his time, Horace Bushnell set the tone for all future discussions of the American home in his widely read discourse "Christian Nurture" (1847). Bushnell makes his mark by reconnecting and then absorbing Emersonian individualism into the value structure of available social institutions. He insists on a dynamic social order rising from the family to the school and church and on to the state. "All society is organic" for Bushnell, and the well-managed home is more than its first "organism"; it is the source of American civilization.

Bushnell, like Emerson, rues "hardness and rudeness" in the bustle of American life, but he counters it with a new concept, "domesticity of character." His theme in "Christian Nurture" is the necessary comfort and intellectual security of the child in the home as it is brought slowly, almost without knowing, to a Christian way of life: "the house, having a domestic Spirit of grace dwelling in it, should become the church of childhood, the table and hearth of a holy rite." Bushnell also insists on a crucial moment in the course of this nurturing process. The first independent understanding of Christianity arrives when the growing child ponders his faith *when left alone* in the comfort of the home. Domesticity supplies the assigned place for solitude in a busy nation— maybe the only place.

But what if there is no home, only a house? That question will guide the chapters that follow. It fixes the American scene of loneliness and, just as significantly, the form literary expression will take. Many an adventure novel supplies a solitary hero, but loneliness is a side theme in it and almost always resolved through plot resolution. When truly gauged, loneliness is not an action. The plight of the lonely is so insidious because it exists quietly in plain sight. It takes its meaning from absence, and the first absence, if not the last, usually comes in loss of home.

The novel of domesticity—domesticity on the edge of dissolution—is therefore our subject. An ignored subgenre in American fiction, it should not be confused with the novel of manners or sentimental fiction. If anything, the novel of disturbed domesticity charts the rupture of a mannered setting into a private level of existence—a level where independent thought controls emotion as the means of recovery and where the quality of reflection defines the character we want to know.

Each of the stories in the next nine chapters revolves around a home lost, partially broken, or in peril. In the wake of these threats, narrative follows the displaced self into the contemplation required for renewal. Failure wrecks a home but gains another through comic relief and wish fulfillment in Chapter 1. Betrayal reduces domesticity to a vainglorious house left empty by those entitled to more in Chapter 2; mere ownership does not make a home. Change helps those who help themselves whether left alone at home or rendered homeless in Chapter 3. Defeat in marriage turns the home into a prison to be unlocked in Chapter 4. In all four of these opening chapters new thought in solitude is both the means and the reward in a narrow escape.

If the home represents the pivotal scene of moral value and educational primacy, as Horace Bushnell claims, it is also a fragile entity with tensions at work hidden from public view. The novel of disturbed domesticity opens the windows of the house for a look into the struggling home. It succeeds by manipulating the contrast between private and public understandings. Incapacity and breakdown undo an already disintegrating home in Chapter 5. Fear and abuse twist domesticity into a battleground in Chapter 6. Prejudice destroys every meaningful domestic relation in Chapter 7. Age and unavoidable loss, the forces that come to even the most successful of homes, enter in Chapters 8 and 9. The dangers and the difficulties in response grow in these later chapters.

Regardless, and despite every problem, despair is never the message. The lords of life must stoop and drop in scale to enter the domestic scene, and they become visible thereby. Against their presence and strength, domesticity on the edge supplies a counterbalance. The home, no matter how broken, is our subject because it is the arena for contemplation and reply. *Alone in America* is about the answering possibilities.

Novels of disturbed domesticity tell us how existence must be managed against the troubles it brings, but they also convey the resources that belong to the realizations in daily life. At bottom, these novels accept the contemplation of self that Emerson demanded as the best guard against the world, but now, more often than not, that self must be fashioned instead of assumed.

For that reason a final chapter, Chapter 10, turns from fiction to the American life that fictionalized itself most successfully around theories of the self. In old age, the poet who made all of America his home, Walt Whitman, gauges the lords of life, and he answers them with craft, honesty, and improvisation. His qualified success hints at what all of us must prepare to do when up against it.

For anyone who would understand America, there are other reasons for continuing to read. Chronologically arranged with some exceptions in chapters where texts are compared across time, each work of fiction defines a cultural moment that provokes the characters we care about onto the page. These characters in conflict with their society serve as witnesses to the problems working themselves through the fabric of the nation. Some of the anxieties they face have been solved, more have not been; but all reveal the problematic role of the individual standing alone against a consensual culture. Where, you might ask, would you take your own stand?

Perhaps this is one place to find out. Stories that matter contain an ingenuity born of need. They demand intricate attention if the story is to give the chance—the chance to look, to reflect, and to claim more than has previously been given. If, in reading, we can say "this is the way it must have been," we have found a truth we can hold. We glimpse a strength of spirit that we might add to our own.

When can a book have such an impact on us? In *Two Cheers for Democracy* (1951), E. M. Forster observes, "The only books that influence us are those for which we are ready, and which have gone a little farther down our path than we have yet gone ourselves." If the books analyzed in the following chapters succeed at this level, it will be because they disrupt domestic scenes in order to push the familiar onto unfamiliar terrain and because the characters who find themselves so estranged must look inward for answers. In effect, American individualism puts every believer somewhere on that separating path with the desire to see farther down it. *Alone in America* welcomes the stories that respond to that need.

The need in itself—almost an obsession in a culture demanding progress—breeds solitary figures everywhere in the literary canon, and readers may miss some of their own favorite examples. Edgar Allan Poe, for one, writes as the most isolated author in all of American culture. His poem "Alone" tells us he has been that way "from childhood's hour," and his stories turn on figures detached from all normal associations. In "The Man without a Country" (1863), Edward Everett Hale creates the most frequently read story in nineteenth-century America by leaving the rebellious Philip Nolan in suspended animation at sea, away from all mention of home and country.

In perhaps the most obvious example of isolation across five novels, James Fenimore Cooper's woodsman is on his own even when companions join him. *The Prairie* (1827) prefigures, in its first pages, Natty Bumppo's singular demise. Unnamed and wasted but enlarged by the setting sun at his back, Leatherstocking at eighty appears "motionless," "musing and melancholy," a "colossal" object of "superstitious awe." He is already ensconced somewhere "between the heavens and the earth." Melville, in turn, invents the term "isolato" to describe Ishmael in *Moby-Dick* (1851) and the lead character in "Bartleby, the Scrivener" (1853), "absolutely alone in the universe," "a bit of wreck in the mid-Atlantic." Kate Chopin is deliberately ambiguous when she leaves Edna Pontellier drowning "in abysses of solitude" as the ultimate outcome of *The Awakening* (1899).

Not to be outdone, twentieth-century fiction glorifies the lonely figures who return home only to reflect on no home found there. Thomas Wolfe's leading novels, *Look Homeward, Angel* (1929) and *You Can't Go Home Again* (1940) take that form. So do Willa Cather's *My Ántonia* (1918) and Robert Penn Warren's *A Place to Come To* (1977). Filled with nostalgia, these modern versions of the isolato must turn inward to recover. Rejecting such solemnity but hitting the same theme with dark humor, Nathanael West's *Miss Lonelyhearts* (1933) parodies loneliness while sustaining it on every page. Sherwood Anderson finds a legion of desperately isolated people in *Winesburg, Ohio* (1919). Few escape the plight he assigns them when we learn "an American town worked terribly at the task of amusing itself."

Many leading twentieth-century protagonists end up adrift. We last see Ernest Hemingway's war heroes forlornly deprived of the loves of their lives in *The Sun Also Rises* (1926), *A Farewell to Arms* (1929), and *For Whom the Bell Tolls* (1940). F. Scott Fitzgerald's seemingly perfect figures fall into flawed isolation. In *The Great Gatsby* (1925), Gatsby waits for the telephone call that will never come: "he must have looked up at an unfamiliar sky through frightening leaves and shivered as he found what a grotesque thing a rose is." Dick Diver knows "the spear had been blunted" but cannot tell when or how it has happened as he begins to disappear in *Tender Is the Night* (1934). Blocked on every side by racism and misunderstanding, the narrator of Ralph Ellison's *Invisible Man* (1952) turns compulsively inward at the end. "I remind myself," he says, "that the true darkness lies within my own mind."

There is a difference between being left in isolation and articulating a positive solution to it. Notably, the lone observer often dominates American poetry, where Emily Dickinson and Robert Frost preside over scores of others, and here the travails and uses of home are often more of a touchstone. The stuttering solitude and challenge in Dickinson's poems depend on her reach from the hidden home to the open universe. "The Angle of a Landscape—," "I felt my life with both my hands," "Alone,

I cannot be—," "I was the slightest in the House—," "They called me to the Window," and many others fill this category. The landscape poems of Robert Frost follow the impulses of "Desert Places," where the scariest empty spaces are at home. "Bereft," "The Door in the Dark," "Tree at My Window," and "The Death of the Hired Man" all revolve around the theme of homes that may only be houses.

If the novel has a philosophical edge over the luminous sparks that lyric poetry can bring to the subject, it lies in the thick descriptions that a faltering domesticity can give to the always changing American scene—a scene that takes away as much as it promises to give. *Alone in America* traces the working out of these puzzles through the sustained thought that formed characters can bring to them.

Even so, there are regrets. Perhaps there should have been room for Dorinda Pedlar in this study. In Ellen Glasgow's *Barren Ground* (1925), Dorinda overcomes the corrosive presence of betrayal in her own home. Grappling for answers that won't come, she concludes that "where beauty exists the understanding soul can never remain desolate." Holden Caulfield might claim a place as well. It is a close call, but the misconceived catcher in the rye perseveres on the run when everyone he encounters turns against him.

Yes, *Barren Ground* and *Catcher in the Rye* (1951) might well have been included. Like the works actually chosen, they celebrate an intimacy of reflection against the problems that come to all of us when dispossessed. On the other hand, the stories in place are representative in particular and perhaps even dominant ways. They are stories we like to read, and there is another reason for that. The writers who create problems within an intricately crafted yet somehow familiar world have a special hold on us. They have learned how to be alone in the act of creation, and that knowledge carries into an understanding of the problems they address. Tracking the familiar into the unfamiliar, they give us glimpses of where we have been, where we are, and where we might have to go.

I

DOES NOBODY HERE KNOW
RIP VAN WINKLE?

Failure has no status in the land of opportunity. How, then, do we explain the first great hero in American literature? For Rip Van Winkle is certainly a failure, even though he succeeds in readers' minds from the moment he walks out of Washington Irving's *Sketch Book* in 1819. Rip somehow turns failure into success. Comic though he is, he also represents an important problem, and it is time to know him better than we do.

"Does nobody here know Rip Van Winkle?" Irving's lonely hero cries when his community turns against him, and the answer has to be that nobody really does. The villagers of his place, Sleepy Hollow, point to another person when the question is asked, and like Irving's millions of readers, they come to enjoy Rip more than they understand him. We hold Rip in esteem because he is a failure that escapes the consequences of failure, and yet his escape is a relief, not an explanation.

Everyone recalls in outline the story of the henpecked husband who walks away from his home into the Kaatskill Mountains to return twenty years later with the excuse that he has just awakened after drinking out of Hendrick Hudson's flagon. Rip has previously allowed his farm to fall into ruin, and he fails to provide for a growing family, which explains the shrewish behavior assigned to his wife. As the explanation of Rip's flight into the mountains, Dame Van Winkle never receives even the courtesy of her full name. The only other trait we learn comes after she is long dead as Rip returns to the shambles of their deserted house, "which, to tell the truth, Dame Van Winkle always kept in neat order."

Irving's description of the lost home is crucial. It tells us that Rip is the half of the couple who has failed to hold up his end. A symbol of America's adolescence and misplaced innocence, he has refused to grow up, and the story he learns to tell on his return allows him to pass from childhood into second childhood without assuming the obligations of maturity in between. Rip, at this superficial level, embodies escapism in a culture driven by diligence, prosperity, and mundane conformity.

These matters have been noted over the years, but surprisingly little attention has been given to the device that makes this hero comic rather than tragic. Lovable Rip trumps irresponsible Rip because he is taken care of! He recovers a home even though he has done nothing to deserve one. Vulnerable and confused on his return to the village, he is destitute, literally helpless. All ends well only when others come to his aid, and the decision to take him back is a narrow one.

Consider, for a moment, an alternative ending that Irving hints at in his story. Once again, the preternaturally old and bewildered Rip returns after twenty years away to a bustling republican town instead of the colonial village that he left without explanation. Here, too, he wears tattered, out-of-date clothes, sports a grizzled unkempt beard, and carries a rusty flintlock.

This Rip is a homeless person and possibly a dangerous one. Again, children and dogs hoot and snarl in his wake, and again he angers the villagers by failing to understand or appreciate the American Revolution that has taken place during his absence. Now, however, the villagers, "a mob at his heels," follow their first inclinations. Instead of helping Rip, they decide to "hustle him" out of town.

In our negative scenario, we have the same uncouth stranger bearing arms on a controversial Election Day, an unwelcome vagrant with no visible means of support. But what if, instead of a saving explanation, village alarm turns into open hostility when Rip unwittingly declares loyalty to King George against "the spirit of '76" and is identified as "a spy"? Many are the villagers in American life today who would act immediately on these fears. We all have neighbors who would spurn Rip as an undesirable alien and send him packing as what Irving himself calls "a Refugee."

We also know from details in the story that Rip is "famished" and that he returns because "it would not do to starve among the mountains." He has no choice but to return, and if forced out of town to beg for his bread, perhaps to die of hunger and exposure, this version of Rip Van Winkle is decidedly tragic, not comic at all.

Irving means for us to glimpse the narrow distance between failure and success. We are to remember that good fortune is often more a matter of luck than self-reliance. It is only "with great difficulty" that a village leader keeps an angry mob from attacking Rip, and the recovery of Rip is deliberately fortuitous. The right individuals must show up in proper sequence for the bewildered Rip to find his way in a community that has easily dismissed all thought of him. The same sequence, all in minor characters, encourages the unreceptive villagers to accept Rip's outlandish tale of hibernation.

Irving quietly floats practical alternatives even as he changes Rip from the lowest pariah into a hero "reverenced as one of the patriarchs." Consider the adroit tag to the story. When some "doubt the reality" of Rip's tale, they wish "that they might have a quieting draught of Rip Van Winkle's flagon." The truth of the matter is that Rip has been an alcoholic on a twenty-year binge. Knowing villagers assign the liquor-filled flagon to Rip and not to mythical nonsense about Hendrick Hudson.

In *The Alcoholic Republic,* W. J. Rorabaugh calculates that liquor consumption per capita in the United States reached its highest point in the first third of the nineteenth century, the same years in which Irving writes his most important fiction, including "Rip Van Winkle." A male drinking cult permeated all levels of society at the time, with the typical village inn getting the lion's share of its business through regulars who gathered to share their liquor, a convivial practice in which every imbiber was expected to buy in turn while passing a flagon around among them.

Endemic drinking is a prominent subject in Irving's satires, and Rip finds his place within this early republican cult of drink. He frequents the local inn whenever possible with "other idle personages" who wile away the hours telling "endless sleepy stories about nothing." The "habits of idleness" would have included his share of drink until he is routed from "the assemblage" by his wife, who, in so doing, breaks the rule of each drinker treating in turn. Her intrusions would have left an imbalance in drinking shares, which surely adds to Rip's public embarrassment and sense of failure.

Irving leaves us with many implications about drink. We learn that Rip Van Winkle is "foremost man in all country frolicks," that his estate has "dwindled away under his management, acre by acre," that he keeps "the worst conditioned farm in the neighbourhood," that his children roam "as ragged and wild as if they belonged to nobody," that matters "grew worse and worse with

Rip Van Winkle," and that Rip is "one of those happy
mortals of foolish, well oiled dispositions."

The code words for a drinker are everywhere in these
descriptions, and they explain Rip's failure and escapism. Drink keeps him from the steady application that
every good farm requires if it is to succeed. Irving plays
with parallels here, and they would have been especially
familiar to his first audiences. He catalogs the same ills
that were regular fodder in temperance tracts from the
period.

Rip's propensities also explain his confrontation with
drink in the Kaatskill Mountains. Hesitant when first
summoned up the hill at twilight by an ominous-looking
stranger dressed in "antique Dutch fashion," Rip joins
anyway when he notes that the stranger "bore on his
shoulder a stout keg that seemed full of liquor." In the
ensuing "frolick" or "evening's gambol," phrases that
suggest regular experience, Rip descends into a fog of
drunkenness:

> He was naturally a thirsty soul and was soon
> tempted to repeat the draught. One taste pro-
> voked another, and he reiterated his visits to
> the flagon so often that at length his senses
> were overpowered, his eyes swam in his head—
> his head gradually declined and he fell into a
> deep sleep.

Rip, like many with a hangover, wakes to blame his
difficulties on "that flagon! That wicked flagon!" Every-

thing after that is the fault of the companions who "dosed him with liquor" before cheating him. Similar to other married men on an extended spree, he then worries about how he will explain himself and his condition to the person that he has let down and ignored. "I shall have a blessed time," he moans, "with Dame Van Winkle." The classic rationalizations of the drinker correspond to Rip's descent from magic in the night into reality of the next day.

The tension between lovable Rip and alcoholic Rip enlivens a whole series of contrasts, and we value Rip because we find our own foibles in him, not because we fear an encounter with Hendrick Hudson. Rip's faults—his laziness, his unconcern, his careless nature, his ability to rationalize away trouble, even his craving for liquor—are our own habits carried to extremes and rendered harmless. The problems of the alcoholic are just as quickly transferred to a nagging wife soon dispensed with.

A communal disappointment at everything he has tried to do, Rip returns at the moment when nothing at all need be done by him! He has "arrived at that happy age when a man can be idle with impunity." Rip therefore resumes "his place once more on the bench at the inn door." But that is not all. Something much more important has happened. Amidst the idle group of regular imbibers, Rip has learned to do one thing extremely well. There at the inn door, where other members are "telling endless sleepy stories about nothing," he tells one with a magical point *about* sleep.

Rip gets the account of his life story right, and it is no mean feat. He is "observed at first to vary on some points, every time he told it," but the man who claims to have been alone for twenty years is not without the resources that solitude can breed. Consulting with no one while gauging reactions, Rip "at last settled down precisely to the tale" that we now hear. Precision is the term of choice here. To get meaning out of "torpor"—Irving's label for the big sleep—requires a philosopher as well as a story-teller. Rip is hardly the first but maybe the best to turn alcoholism into a magic tale.

The teller *is* the story, but he learns how to get others to accept it and him with pleasure. Control of one's life story is not to be sneezed at as one form of happiness. The crux of this remarkable accomplishment lies in the thinking man's ability to step back and see what he has become and to then mold it into usable form. Who can resist the satisfaction in this dual accomplishment? To fashion personal success out of public failure is the stuff of dreams. Who in this fallen world could ask for more?

The fallen world is, in fact, everywhere in "Rip Van Winkle," and it adds to Irving's appeal. *The Sketch Book* thrives on the softening of the darker facts in the life cycle. Irving is a master at turning pessimism into song. Grieving mothers, dead sons, jilted lovers, sailors lost at sea, disgraced bankrupts, and funerals proliferate in *The Sketch Book,* with "Rip Van Winkle" as its center-piece. Irving casts every problem into sentiment, where vicarious sorrow overwhelms the nasty particulars.

Rip is indeed a shiftless alcoholic, an addict who shirks the obligations of house and home, but Diedrich Knickerbocker, the ancient historian who narrates Irving's story, "winks" these negative traits into the imaginary past of Sleepy Hollow, a place we can regard with interest without having to care about it.

Still, the "wink" in Winkle is also on us. Every reader soon grasps that Rip presents contemporary problems as well as past foibles. Irving even had a term for the twists that he gave to the troubles in life. In an earlier satire, *Salmagundi* (1807), he called his method "the whim-whams," where the "whim" softens the "wham." Grim realities become antic qualities in Irving's fiction. We laugh because we recognize everyday problems without having to deal with them.

"Rip Van Winkle" works in this way but also at a deeper level of concern that touches every American. The terrors in life that Irving addresses and Rip experiences are the basic ones we all must deal with. Figuratively speaking, Rip has died and come back to life on his own terms, thwarting a community that has consigned him to oblivion. Rip, in this vein, is every oldster who feels left behind in a changing society.

Irving illustrates this side of the problem by turning his protagonist into nothing in just twenty years. All of the returning vagabond's important peers have passed away during Rip's curious hiatus, and the few insignificant ones who remain are of no account in a rapidly changing society. When Rip goes to sleep as a colonial subject and awakens as a citizen of the state of New York in ignorance of republican ways, the discrepancies make him a type for every passing generation's failure to adapt and keep pace amidst the suddenly shifting sands of the democratic experiment.

Rip discovers that his neighbors have no interest in bringing him back to life! He returns an irrelevancy. He has died twice, once in the sleep on the mountain—really in the drinking holes of upstate New York—and next in the perception of Sleepy Hollow. But Rip, so carefully named by Irving, cannot "Rest In Peace." Suddenly and awkwardly alive in front of his angry and astonished neighbors, he loses all identity in the face of their resentment: "I can't tell what's my name or who I am!"

Irving dramatizes the way the present ruthlessly rejects the past by having Rip ask for the "patriarch of the village":

> Rip bethought himself a moment and enquired, "Where's Nicholaus Vedder?" There was a silence for a little while, when an old man replied, in a thin, piping voice, "Nicholaus Vedder? Why he is dead and gone these eighteen years! There was a wooden tombstone in the church yard that used to tell all about him, but that's rotted and gone too."

The past is "rotted and gone." A quavering figure remembers it but only grudgingly and in dismissive tones.

Stripped of every connection, Rip finds "himself thus alone in the world," and in that enforced loneliness he begins to sink. Here is the crisis that almost every protagonist in American literature experiences at some point. The often intolerant consensual spirit of democratic culture leads to primal fear of public rejection. Loneliness without connection or resource keyed to communal antipathy is about to destroy Rip. He has been relegated to a history that no one wants to remember. Inconveniently back, he belongs with the forgotten dead, where he is spoken of in formulaic negative terms: "poor man . . . whether he shot himself, or was carried away by the Indians nobody can tell."

This moment is where the deeper story takes hold. Nobody can tell what happened to Rip, and no one in the village has cared enough to find out. The situation in this instant is neither comic nor tragic but somewhere in between. Pushed so casually out of common existence, Rip must struggle to re-create himself. He belongs in the past, a feckless failure that no one wants to remember. The youthful present is his enemy, and he must battle against it as a phenomenon hostile to his very existence.

Not the least handicap of the returning man, one that must be turned into an advantage for Rip to survive, has to do with his age. How old is Rip? As with another famous isolated figure in American literature, Ishmael in *Moby-Dick,* his exact age is left to conjecture, but returning Rip needs that distinction, and it comes in a desperate familial claim: "'I am your father!' cried he—'Young Rip Van Winkle once—old Rip Van Winkle now! Does nobody know poor Rip Van Winkle?'"

As the father of a young family, Rip could have been no more than thirty-five at the time of his disappearance, which makes him fifty-five at most and probably younger on his return. Nonetheless, his plight calls for helpless old age in a declaration of dependence. In the act of self-naming, his claim of fatherhood, "poor Rip" fuses pity with the corollary of care. The status he must avoid at all costs is middle age with its vocational responsibilities. He was young *then* but must appear old *now* to obtain the assistance he needs.

Rip thus represents the plight of every old person who has lost track of the world, with generational tensions at work. Three versions of Rip Van Winkle appear in the story. Rip, the returning father, is matched by Rip, the son, who looks and acts exactly like his father when the first Rip disappeared into the Kaatskills, but this second Rip contemplates the return of his father with indifference. Finally, there is Rip, the baby grandson, who cries in fear in his first encounter with the long-lost grandfather.

More than humor is at work in these confused identities. Returning Rip, the father, panics at the sight of his indifferent son: "that's me yonder—no—that's somebody else got into my shoes." Stunned out of his identity, he draws the connection he needs only by recognizing his crying grandson. Since all Rips are lazily alike in their self-absorption, no Rip helps any other Rip, but the third Rip, held in his mother's arms, unwittingly restores the first Rip to his place in Sleepy Hollow.

This sequence has a certain logic to it. Many a grandparent and grandchild know the magic in a skipped generation. There is, in any event, a more direct link, and it represents the hidden factor in transmissions. In Irving's story her name is Judith Gardenier, the keeper of the garden, so named, and as Rip's daughter she appears only in this highly charged and completely restricted moment.

One can imagine a feminist account of this story entitled "Does Anyone Know Judith Gardenier?" "A fresh likely looking woman" with her baby in her arms, Judith has "pressed through the throng to get a peep at the greybearded man" who is so rudely interrogated by the crowd, and she soon pays for her curiosity. She is termed "fresh" because new to the story, and she is "likely" because absolutely needed for Irving's plot resolution. When her child, the third Rip, cries, she admonishes him. "'Hush Rip,' cried she, 'hush you little fool, the old man won't hurt you.'"

Old Rip is saved by these words. He hears "the name of the child, the air of the mother, the tone of her voice," so like the previous scolding tones of his dead wife, and promptly makes the claim that justifies his place in her lineage: "I am your father!" A strange, gray-bearded curiosity no longer, he has become the aged and deserving parent who by every familial right must be taken into his daughter's home.

To cement Judith Gardenier's obligation in the social terms needed, Irving introduces several of his creatures, starting with another woman, this one unnamed but uncannily useful in a cameo appearance. "An old woman tottering out from among the crowd" recognizes Rip, verifies his claim to identity, justifies his return, and disappears as quickly as she came. "Sure enough!" she confirms, "it is Rip Van Winkle—it is himself—welcome home again old neighbor—why, where have you been these twenty long years?"

Where *has* he been? The question in the tottering woman's welcome demands an immediate answer for Rip to be accepted on good terms, and Irving responds by conjuring up an equally old village historian who excuses Rip on the spot. This second elderly figure, almost as ephemeral as the last, tells the ghostly legend of Hendrick Hudson's return every twenty years in support of Rip's story.

Rip can be irresponsible, but he cannot have intended his disappearance from the village. Otherwise daughter Judith exists not just as a mother with a child but as a deserted child herself. Realistically, Judith Gardenier *is* that deserted child. Unnamed until this moment, she has been one of Rip's impoverished brood, and she has grown up like the rest of them "as ragged and wild as if they belonged to nobody." Judith has raised herself not through her family but by the traditional mechanism of the clever young woman: she has married well. She owes nothing but a childhood of pain to her father.

Irving knows better than to encourage this narrative of parental neglect, but he wants us to glimpse it, "the wham" within "the whim." Priority, though, belongs to the old people in his story. His subject is a hero grown suddenly old, one who cannot solve his plight alone even if, manifestly, he *is* alone.

Old Rip, the tottering woman who confirms his identity, and the ancient historian who authenticates his story belong to the same generation, and they join forces to make youth serve them in their need. Not for the last time, elders band together to protect themselves from their progeny in a youth culture. Their efforts amount to a rearguard action against assumptions of irrelevancy. They respond to what Thomas Cole in his study of the aging process, *The Journey of Life,* terms "the demeaning of aging rooted in modern culture's relentless hostility toward decay and dependency."

The resonances here carry across the centuries. The problem of growing old in a youth culture will vex each future American generation when no longer young, and it will percolate in the rationale of many stories to come. Rip sets the stage because he is young and, in the wink of an eye, disastrously old. He is the precursor of all aged characters in American fiction, some of whom will appear later in this volume. These seemingly useless and often lonely oldsters appear strangely out of place in a country thought to be young, but curiously they are also the measure and gauge of it. They are the problem that comes to all who live long enough in a nation changing out from under everyone, and their story recurs so frequently because there is no answer except oblique recognition of it.

Comic resolution, the mask in "Rip Van Winkle," depends on the dutiful daughter taking her helpless father into her "snug, well furnished house." Thus provided for, Rip enjoys a renewed life of idleness but now with unalloyed pleasure, and he brings new control to it as both the owner *and* the teller of a marvelous life story. Judith Gardenier, for her part, cares for her father without complaint because she must in confirmation of communal understandings. As Robert Frost writes so poignantly in "The Death of the Hired Man," "Home is the place where, when you have to go there, / They have to take you in."

Just the same, Irving's solution is not without a complication. Rip detects his wife's asperity when his daughter scolds her child ("that tone of her voice"), and his recognition introduces one more meaning, a nugget of realism and another irony in Irving's story. Judith's waspish reprimand—"Hush, Rip . . . hush, you little fool, the old man won't hurt you"—saves old Rip, who occupies the logical parallel of old fool. But do Judith's words mean that she might be shrewish like her mother? And what of the youngest Rip? Are his mother's words true? Is it true that "the old man" can't hurt him?

Each generation of Rip Van Winkle is exactly like the one before except for an ominous detail. Each Rip is less than the one that came before him. Old Rip owned a farm; his son Rip, "the ditto of himself," carries on in laziness, but he has less to start with and ends up as a hired hand working another's land. Downward mobility applies to every pleasure-seeking Rip that we have seen.

How many idle Rips will be able to duplicate old Rip's escape, an escape that he has done nothing to earn beyond the telling of it? Disaster awaits every new Rip who fails to find a nurturing female to solve his situation. The littlest and latest Rip in Irving's story faces this prospect, and it is no wonder that he cries out in alarm at what he sees. Nor is that his only problem in the return of his drunken grandfather. Will Mother Judith have the time, the means, and the patience to take care of both of them?

When the littlest Rip cries at the sight of his decrepit and helpless grandfather, he is a part of Irving's comedy, but he is no fool as the symbol of an anxious future. Baby Rip cries in a growing line of child men who must find someone to take care of them. Of course, anyone can rest in the story at the level of Irving's whimsy, but the underlying myth of Rip has a more tenacious grip, and its hidden power explains why this story survives the centuries. A lonely man consumed by failure through addiction to drink is miraculously taken care of and even honored for it in a country that worships only success.

"Rip Van Winkle" succeeds by loading time in favor of its hero and therefore in favor of us. The shiftless vagrant who limps out of the hills enjoys astounding good fortune. He also seizes the moment. He converts failure into success on his own terms, and how he does it is inspiring. Rip takes control of his story in a way that few manage to do. His creative rebirth against all logic holds every audience. Twin elements endear him to us. He represents the power of imagination at work in a crisis; also the hope that help will come when we ourselves are left alone to face the torments of existence.

2

NATHANIEL HAWTHORNE
DISSECTS BETRAYAL

The connoisseur of betrayal in American literature is Nathaniel Hawthorne, though he is seldom identified in this way. Three of the four major novels—*The Scarlet Letter, The House of the Seven Gables,* and *The Blithedale Romance*—turn on the subject. So do many of the most powerful short stories: "Ethan Brand," "Wakefield," "Alice Doane's Appeal," "The Birthmark," "The Gentle Boy," "Young Goodman Brown," "Rappaccini's Daughter," and "My Kinsman, Major Molineux."

Hawthorne called these stories romances, by which he meant works that brought together different levels of reality with an intensity that heightened both. Trust proceeds at one level of truth, an ideal one; betrayal works on another, down where the dog-eared mechanics of life exist. Hawthorne brought the two levels together as art. He understood that to be betrayed is to be undone by life itself. He also realized the answers to it had to come again from life and not from any of the explanations offered for it.

A near recluse as a young man, Hawthorne knew loneliness as well as the need to be alone. He wrote as one of the first to see how deeply that tension is woven into the fabric of American life, and he made betrayal his favorite device for exploring the distance in between. Deception through personal contact supplies the trauma in his stories, an emphasis all the more painful to an author who also believed that meaning had to come through the integrity of human relationships.

"My Kinsman, Major Molineux," to take up the examples to be used here, clarifies the reasons for betrayal, while *The House of the Seven Gables* concentrates on the plight of the betrayed. Hawthorne is ruthlessly precise in both instances, and he insists on peculiarly American components in his theme. Personal devastation always comes with a level of communal duplicity in his stories.

In "My Kinsman, Major Molineux," written in 1832, a "shrewd" country boy arrives in the city to seek his fortune. The opening replicates rags-to-riches stories already entrenched in American thought, but Hawthorne turns the conventional quest on its head with an ending that still mystifies readers today. Young Robin—his surname can only be inferred—has come to the city to make his way through a rich relative, Major Molineux. There is no prospect of a return home; only what will turn out to be the false prospect of a new home. An older brother will inherit all there is in the country, and their father, a village parson, has sent Robin on his way with "half the remnant of his last year's salary," the only patrimony Robin will ever receive. He proceeds utterly alone.

The urban dwellers that Robin soon meets greet his request for Major Molineux with mysterious sneers, curses, threats, rudeness, and laughter. Touches of violence color these encounters. Hawthorne, being Hawthorne, uses the device to lead his adventurer through each of the seven deadly sins—anger, avarice, envy, gluttony, lust, sloth, and pride—saving the last for Robin's false pride over the family connection.

In the end, a seemingly amiable observer holds Robin on the street "to witness" the boy's reaction when Major Molineux, "an elderly man, of large, and majestic person," is carried past them tarred and feathered by a howling mob. All we learn about this beleaguered kinsman is that he has "strong, square features, betokening a steady soul"—features needed as he tries to hold up against "overwhelming humiliation" and "tremendous ridicule." Hawthorne assigns no sin or crime to Major Molineux. No justification is given for the "foul disgrace of a head that had grown grey in honor."

Our sympathies therefore move from Hawthorne's bewildered protagonist to the elderly person subjected to public outrage. For whether he deserves such treatment or not, the victim of the mob is steadfast under horrible treatment. Major Molineux remains "majestic still in his agony" to the bitter end of the story. The mob is what Hawthorne condemns, not the man: "on they went in counterfeited pomp, in senseless uproar, in frenzied merriment, trampling all on an old man's heart."

The strange turn in the story comes here. Robin has been laughed at repeatedly during his progress through town, and now, with his knees shaking and hair bristling in "pity and terror," he is laughed at again more openly and collectively by the same merrymakers who mocked him in earlier encounters. Everyone in town enjoys the shock of recognition that passes between the humiliated kinsman and the boy who can no longer seek his help. Suddenly, though, again with no explanation given, Robin joins the laughter of the mob, and his laughter rings loudest and longest of all—so loud and so long, in fact, that he knows his kinsman "will scarce desire to see my face again."

What has happened here, and what is left to Robin? Defeated, bewildered, and ready to return to the rural home that is now lost to him, he is stopped again by the calculating observer who has paused with such "singular curiosity to witness your meeting." This self-satisfied voyeur, "a gentleman in his prime," plays upon the term that Hawthorne has used throughout to describe Robin: his "shrewdness." The same ambiguous figure also gets the last word: "Perhaps, as you are a shrewd youth, you may rise in the world, without the help of your kinsman, Major Molineux."

There are several facets to Robin's laughter. The fall of Major Molineux proves that no generation really helps another in a country of rapid change and rampant individualism. With no established moral dimension, the Major appears to us as merely old, irrelevant, and cast aside—an anachronism in contrast to the "gentleman in his prime." Robin laughs here in dismissal of a lost frame of reference and in bewilderment as we often do when amazed by a sudden change in fortune. Like the mob, his laughter also responds to public comeuppance of the great, a comic story often told in American culture.

Deeper currents make the laughter loud, and they are more sinister. "Laughter when out of place, mistimed, or bursting forth from a disordered state of feeling may be the most terrible modulation of the human voice," Hawthorne writes in "Ethan Brand," another story on the theme of betrayal. This claim exactly describes the manifestation we find in "My Kinsman, Major Molineux." Why does Robin laugh with such disordered feeling and in such an unmodulated, prolonged way?

The answer to this question encompasses all others. Hawthorne has maneuvered the once confident Robin into "a sensation of loneliness" that makes his world disintegrate around him. "Oh, that any breathing thing were here with me!" Robin moans. "Am I here or there?"

he cries again. Long gone is the bold quester who walked into town with "as light a step" and "as eager an eye" as could be imagined.

Robin laughs in such a distorted fashion out of the need to belong somewhere, and the easiest way to reconnect is to betray his kinsman and laugh with those who have laughed at him. It is telling that he adopts the cruelty of the mob without sharing any of its reasons. He laughs to cover his own loneliness and lack of inner resources.

All of the explanations previously offered for Robin's laughter come together in this bottomless fear of loneliness. To be separated from all you know, to have no peers, to be lost during a journey, to be shunned by all, to be laughed at by everyone, to plan for success and have it publicly ridiculed, to see a chosen hero disgraced, to belong nowhere, to be homeless without resources, to have no plan except retreat, to have been exposed in a foolish mistake, to not understand, to feel betrayed by life itself—these are the elements that drive us into levels of loneliness that become intolerable.

But if loneliness comes to all, Hawthorne's story underscores its pernicious attributes in American culture. Readers who appear perplexed by "My Kinsman, Major Molineux" ignore the social reality it depicts. The flip side of a vaunted self-reliance in America is fear of dismissal by a consensual culture.

Sociologist David Riesman identified this phenomenon half a century ago in *The Lonely Crowd*. "Other-directedness" trumps "inner-directedness" in his "Study of the Changing American Character," and the two states of mind create opposing behavior patterns. When other-directed individuals like Robin cannot look within themselves, they join the crowd that has made them feel lonely in the first place.

The intrinsic unreliability of this crowd is as much a subject of Riesman's study as it is in Hawthorne's story. The price paid for joining the crowd can be high. Robin is not "shrewd," as claimed. We don't hear from him except through his mistakes, misunderstanding, and confusion. In the last sentence of *The Lonely Crowd,* Riesman delivers his most confident conclusion about other-directed people: "they lose their social freedom and their individual autonomy in seeking to become like each other."

Hawthorne exposes tragic undercurrents in the comic story of upward mobility. The seeming smoothness of other-directed success should not disguise its jagged edges. Given the need to join, what group does one seek and with what level of commitment? To join masks the fear of being alone, but joining brings new fears. How, asks the joiner, do I keep my place? Is this the right group? How is the group doing? What if I am no longer needed? When will I be cast adrift?

Fear of betrayal creates its own loneliness and a corresponding ugliness in human nature. It fuels the impulse to betray in the name of the group to avoid being deceived and undone by it. The truest American story is thus only superficially about slaying the foe. Its deeper reach depicts an isolated figure against a hostile crowd. The one against the many, rather than from many one, describes the essence of a community shaped by leveling impulses and that rarely knows its own mind.

Hawthorne is the master of this scene. In "My Kinsman, Major Molineux," Robin enters a world that has no place for him on the terms that have been assigned to him, not an infrequent occurrence in a changing American society. Held conspicuously apart and in danger of being absorbed on the losing side of a confrontation, he must either challenge or accept the disapproval of those around him. As we saw in "Rip Van Winkle," the crisis of the American story comes in such moments.

The comic improbabilities of "Rip Van Winkle" allow Rip to rejoin his group, and he does it by creating a new identity all his own. "My Kinsman, Major Molineux" insists on the choice between one or the other. We are left on the cusp of twin possibilities: either the separate integrity of the self or a shared identity with the group. Hawthorne dangles the alternatives without a resolution in order to prove the pattern. The predicament of loneliness and its potential answers (coming either from within or arranged through pressure from without) are obsessive concerns in American literature, and they define character through the difficulty of the choice to be made.

That choice is always a close call in an interesting story, and the narrative of isolation responds by testing whether a deeper understanding of self can resolve the crisis. The typical answer to this uncertainty comes in plot resolution, the element deliberately withheld in "My Kinsman, Major Molineux," but if Hawthorne's manipulation of final ambiguity is unusual for the 1830s, it rests on a mystery frequently invoked but typically unanswered in American fiction.

What is the source, the inner makeup, that allows the solitary self to choose as it does? What, in the chronicle of isolation, controls the difference between someone standing alone and someone lonely and vulnerable? The question is harder to answer than it should be in a literature that gives so much attention to the theme of individualism, and the difficulty has an underlying basis. For no matter how one approaches the subject, the theory of self-reliance in American culture is intellectually thin. It is an ideological boast or call to arms more than an informed or articulated philosophical conception.

Hawthorne's most extended story of betrayal, *The House of the Seven Gables,* exposes the limits of self-reliance by proving how much we depend on others for meaning. Every act of trust in Hawthorne is fraught with danger. Those few people that we might trust are surrounded by many more who are not to be relied on in a culture without a safety net. The betrayals that isolate Hawthorne's characters burn inward, but they flourish in a competitive society controlled by wealth and influence.

Hawthorne writes his novel in 1850 with publication in 1851 as regional accusations dominate a nation struggling to preserve itself with hypocritical solutions. The Compromise of 1850, one of a series of immoral bargains over the thriving institution of slavery, pleases neither side in heightened sectional strife, and many northerners feel betrayed by the strengthened Fugitive Slave Act that it contains. Hawthorne shows his awareness by making his angriest characters swallow "Jim Crow" cookies.

It is one thing to be persecuted by a tyrannical regime; another to be wrongly penalized by a community that likes to think of itself as just. Being robbed of freedom may have its uses, but what if it is enforced on an innocent person for thirty years, as it is in Hawthorne's story, or imposed on every slave who managed to live that long?

Clifford Pyncheon, at the center of *The House of the Seven Gables,* has been driven half crazy by decades of false imprisonment. He has been convicted in court on another's perjured testimony, and the betrayer is a member of his own family, as well as a judge in the legal system. Familial conflict and legal implication replicate the fratricidal disputes that are driving the United States apart.

Hawthorne focuses on the long aftermath of betrayal. As in "Rip Van Winkle" before it, and as in so many other early American stories, *The House of the Seven Gables* gestures toward youth in a story that is really about damaged old people. With a limited past and a disturbing present, nineteenth-century Americans wondered whether time was on their side or running out. The symbol of their anxiety is Clifford Pyncheon, and he can only be saved by miraculous intervention.

Imbued with these contextual anxieties, *The House of the Seven Gables* is now relegated to secondary status. *The Scarlet Letter* may be more popular today because *The House of the Seven Gables* strikes more directly and uncomfortably at ongoing problems in American culture. As Hawthorne told his editor James T. Fields, this second novel required "more care and thought." *The Scarlet Letter* reaches back to the original settlements of Puritans over sin and guilt. Though haunted by the Puritan past, *The House of the Seven Gables* is set in the authorial present. It explores immediate and still relevant social issues: control by the rich, greed, economic flux, dispossession, intransigence, and corruption fill its pages.

The philosophical heft is also more insistent here. Someone dies in *The Scarlet Letter. The House of the Seven Gables* probes death itself and the import of it in generational scrambles for inherited wealth. Two villains stoke conflict. Judge Jaffrey Pyncheon uses false testimony to betray his cousin and rival for the family legacy. Supporting him in very important ways are the forces of public opinion, which engage in levels of malice and prejudice that are much harder to explain.

The difficult problem belongs to this second level. Hawthorne kills off Jaffrey Pyncheon easily enough, but death creates more problems than it solves when the judge's ally, the angry life of the street, has no ability or interest in finding the truth. The seven gables of the house mark off the decades from the founding of the nation, and Hawthorne doesn't like what they have produced. Materialism and political cowardice have twisted the republic and dulled the sensibilities of its citizens.

In the most dramatic chapter of the novel, "The Scowl and Smile," Hepzibah Pyncheon tries to protect her brother Clifford from their grasping cousin Jaffrey. Hawthorne uses the scene to question a culture that has sacrificed elemental notions of fairness to material success as the gauge of meaning:

> Yet how continually it comes to pass, thought Hepzibah, in this dull delirium of a world—that whosoever, and with however kindly a purpose, should come to help, they would be sure to help the strongest side! Might and wrong combined, like iron magnetized, are endowed with irresistible attraction.

The passage describes a nation manipulating legal artifice to sustain slavery and, through it, the commercial well-being of the prosperous.

The retrospective conceit of *The House of the Seven Gables* captures the unresolved problem in national origins. An omniscient narrator opens the story by insisting on the hold of the past in tones that are Sophoclean. As in Greek tragedy, a curse on previous generations leads to familial disintegration. Hawthorne equates this downward spiral to the justification of slavery in the founding of the republic: "The wrong-doing of one generation lives into the successive ones, and divesting itself of every temporary advantage, becomes a pure and uncontrollable mischief."

The original curse is simple enough in plot terms. The first Pyncheon in America, a colonel and leader of the original colony, displaces Matthew Maule, a man of lesser rank who owns desirable land in the town of Salem. Pyncheon has Maule condemned for witchcraft. From the scaffold, the convicted wizard responds, "God will give him blood to drink!" And God does. The Colonel dies of blood-spurting apoplexy as soon as he completes the house he has built on Maule's land.

A curse adheres to place as well as persons, so each new generation of Pyncheon possessors suffers through the unfair gains and the negative traits of its forebear. Avarice, lust, gluttony, selfishness, and pride control the unjust possessors of the property; the house on it is never really a home. Meanwhile, the progeny of the betrayed deform themselves. The dispossessed descendants of Matthew Maule twist their own lives by gloating over the misery of their enemies. Class warfare percolates across the generations, and the present as much as the past allows villainy to thrive.

It is crucial in this conflict that Jaffrey Pyncheon is already wealthy far beyond need. The Judge has the same unbounded greed as the original Colonel, and he threatens the recently paroled Clifford with new incarceration if Clifford will not divulge what he knows of ancient familial claims to Indian lands. Jaffrey is passionate but delusional in this regard. As the most prominent leader in his community, he personifies a national failing: no American ever seems to have enough money and always wants more of it.

The pathology of betrayal through greed and uncertainty appears in an opening comment about the rise and fall of family fortunes. "In this republican country, amid the fluctuating waves of our social life," Hawthorne explains, "somebody is always at the drowning point." And no one cares. A citizen who rejects material advance as success amidst such uncertainty—as Uncle Venner, a minor character, decides to do in chapter four—appears "rather deficient, than otherwise, in his wits." Thirst for gain and fear of decline in an economy of boom and bust encourages ruthlessness in relationships, and Jaffrey Pyncheon typifies the phenomenon in American culture.

Clifford has been betrayed first by Jaffrey, his cousin, and then by a corrupt legal system. Hepzibah, the other formal possessor of the house, suffers from fallen status and poverty. In the rote terms of the curse, they continue to pay as Pyncheons who occupy the wrongfully possessed property of the Maules.

An otherwise aimless adventurer named Holgrave completes the circle. In disguise he rents rooms in the house to probe the miseries of the Pyncheons as the last in a cold-blooded line of Maules. This secret voyeur hovering over the domestic collapse of the Pyncheons is creepy enough to serve on both sides of the problematics of betrayal. In "Alice Pyncheon," he will mesmerize but not complete the violation of a Pyncheon lady as a more unscrupulous Maule has done in the past.

Hawthorne breaks the cycle of pain through a traditional marriage of opposites. He brings a conveniently orphaned country cousin, Phoebe Pyncheon, into the house, and although Phoebe is as careful to make money as any of her covetous forebears, she is sufficiently distinct to serve as a logical bride. Significantly, she enters the novel homeless and must find one. Her marriage to the cleaned-up Holgrave blunts the curse by joining the Pyncheons and the Maules in domestic bliss.

But not quite. The pulse of the novel, Hawthorne's critical assessment of America, keeps its own time. Every seeming plot resolution at the level of the curse creates a new problem at one remove. Hawthorne's happy ending barely covers a host of troubling issues. Holgrave, symbol of "the artist" in a chapter titled "The Daguerreotypist," reveals what is philosophically at stake for Hawthorne:

> Only this is such an odd and incomprehensible
> world! The more I look at it, the more it puzzles
> me; and I begin to suspect that a man's bewil-
> derment is the measure of his wisdom. Men
> and women, and children, too, are such strange
> creatures, that one never can be certain that he
> really knows them; nor ever guess what they
> have been, from what he sees them to be, now.

Acts of betrayal between "strange creatures" in "an odd and incomprehensible world" would seem to be normal occurrences. This view of things comes from the man consumed by his knowledge of treachery in the Pyncheon line, and Hawthorne underlines its significance by leaving no one in the house of gables at the end. Desertion of the prize so many have fought over for so long would seem to make no sense in a story about inheritance and the right to possess property. On the other hand, the abandoned house that is no home symbolizes the loneliness and despair in betrayal that throbs at the heart of the novel.

Every character is plunged into either the knowledge or the danger of betrayal at some point in Hawthorne's story, but the ravages of it are best seen in the two characters who are forced to live it obsessively: Clifford Pyncheon has been sentenced through it, and Holgrave uses it for nefarious reasons.

In "The Pyncheon Garden," the impact of unjust incarceration on Clifford Pyncheon furnishes the contemplative center of the novel. Clifford has been smashed into incoherence by the perfidy in events. "All his life long, he had been learning how to be wretched, as one learns a foreign language." Lest we miss the general relevance, Hawthorne makes this wretchedness emblematic rather than specific:

> He [Clifford] was an example and representative of that great chaos of people, whom an inexplicable Providence is constantly putting at cross-purposes with the world; breaking what seems its own promise in their nature; withholding their proper food, and setting poison before them for a banquet; and thus—when it might so easily, as one would think, have been adjusted otherwise—making their existence a strangeness, a solitude, and torment.

These words suggest that betrayal exists in the very promise of life and that estrangement and torment come to all. "Fate," the narrator intrudes to tell Clifford, "has no happiness in store for you." Nor for anyone who survives long enough! "Alas, poor Clifford. You are old, and worn with troubles that ought never to have befallen you. You are partly crazy and partly imbecile; a ruin, a failure, as almost everybody is—though some in less degree, or less perceptibly than their fellows."

Almost everybody a ruin? A failure? There is no end to the misery Hawthorne wants to make us see through this one betrayed life. The subject comes up again in the last pages of the novel. For Clifford, or anyone seriously victimized, "there is no reparation." Hawthorne refuses to minimize the horror when lives are betrayed, and he turns the observation into an abstract truth about the ways of the world: "No great mistake, whether acted or endured, in our mortal sphere is ever really set right. . . . If after long lapse of years, the right seems to be in our power, we find no niche to set it in."

All of this happens because people easily tolerate a level of injustice when it is imposed on others. In *The House of the Seven Gables,* the toleration of slavery in a free republic confirms a general moral indifference. Out of habit, advantage, prejudice, or simple avoidance, even a presumably just society will accept the wrongful acts of the past as part of the regular and ordinary dispensations in life.

The tenacity of wrongful acts takes center stage in the chapter "The Scowl and Smile." For the only time in the novel, two intellectual equals battle toe to toe in a demonstration of how people deceive themselves at the expense of others to gain a competitive advantage. Predictably, no saving clarity emerges from the struggle. Jaffrey and Hepzibah Pyncheon quarrel over Clifford's fate, and Jaffrey's hard tactics overwhelm Hepzibah's vague moral challenge. For even though Jaffrey fails, the outside world sides with him even after he has failed, and more than ignorance explains the world's preference.

A reader naturally pulls for Hepzibah in this conflict, but her position is too frightening for the average
sensibility to accept as evil unhinges understanding
and destroys all sense of balance. Even the scales of
justice betray their purpose; they reward the powerful,
not the innocent or those in need. "What is there so pon-
derous in evil," mourns the narrator, "that a thumb's
bigness of it should outweigh the mass of things not
evil, which were heaped in the other scale!"

The depth of Jaffrey's depravity is exposed in "The
Scowl and Smile," but it cannot be encompassed or
fronted, and Hepzibah's desperation forces her toward
deeper registers. Too bitter to pray, she invokes the deity
anyway. "God will not let you do the thing you medi-
tate!" she warns. Jaffrey has forgotten in his renewed
attack on the helpless man he has already destroyed
that "there ever was affection between man and man, or
pity from one man to another in this miserable world!"
And to what end? "You are not young Cousin Jaffrey—no
nor middle-aged—but already an old man," Hepzibah
cries. "The hair is white upon your head! How many
years have you to live?"

The literal answer to Hepzibah's question comes immediately and gives her what she needs to stop Jaffrey,
but the implications of her words reach far beyond the
situation. Jaffrey dies from the family disease of apoplexy not years but minutes later in the house where so
many before him have "mused, slumbered, and departed,

to a yet profounder sleep." "Time flies!" the Judge declares in his last moment of life. Yes, it does, and it continues to fly in existential terror once flown.

Death is an ambiguous servant in this scene. Jaffrey's sudden end gives everything to his enemies. Hepzibah and Clifford, his generational rivals, inherit his estate, but while plot needs are resolved in the dispatch of Jaffrey, Hepzibah's agonized question—"How many years have you to live?"—floats on. Her words give years or *less* to all of us, and they poison all of human endeavor.

The narrator ponders the fatalistic import in this situation by mocking Jaffrey's thwarted ambitions. Question after derisive question falls unanswered on the dead man in "Governor Pyncheon," and readers naturally join in glee over the demise of a villain. Gradually, though, the narrator's questions plunge out of control and philosophically toward something quite different and terrible.

We all die figuratively in this scene. The narrator's dance over Jaffrey's corpse ends with a fly creeping toward the open eyeballs of the dead man. "Where is our universe?" asks Hawthorne. "All crumbled away from us; and we, adrift in chaos, may hearken to the gusts of homeless wind that go sighing and murmuring about, in quest of what was once a world!" Everyone meets Jaffrey's fate. Our personal "bubble," like Jaffrey's in "The Departure," will burst into the same "vacancy" as just another "momentary eddy." Hawthorne's "homeless wind" delivers us to no place.

The philosophical holder of this dark vision and the second figure trapped in a symbiosis of loneliness and betrayal is, as his name implies, Holgrave, a connection underlined by the singular absence of a first name. In "The Flower of Eden," as an organ grinder plays merry tunes outside the room of the dead Jaffrey, Holgrave endures the worst hour of his life. He has accepted the demand of his forebears that he witness for the betrayed and relish the pain of the usurping Pyncheons. The keeper of Maule's curse, he has been photographing the corpse, and it is too much for him. Whatever pleasure he extracts from the ruin of his enemy devolves into "a scene of guilt, and of retribution more dreadful than the guilt."

Retribution seems beside the point when death comes no matter what the quality of the life. Jaffrey, looked at in this way, has received an easier death than most; certainly easier than he deserves. Fear, fear of death, belongs to the observer in this scene, not the recipient. Holgrave's pleasure in the now helpless betrayer plunges him into "shapeless gloom." He enters a world where the betrayal of mortality is king, and it is a "strange, wild, evil, hostile" scene, where he, not Jaffrey, is the lonely one.

Knowledge of the whole grave has come to match Holgrave's condition as well as his name. "The sense of it took away my youth," he says. "I never hoped to feel young again!" Just in time, Phoebe, symbol of "The Flower of Eden," supplies the necessary antidote when she reappears in the house, but Hawthorne will not leave it there. Only those who are strong enough to face death see beyond it. Holgrave's expression of this truth is muted but plain: "The world owes all its onward impulse to men ill at ease."

Hawthorne pulls us out of so much negation with the most daring plot twist in all of nineteenth-century American literature; he has Holgrave and Phoebe declare their love over the festering corpse of Jaffrey Pyncheon. "The image of awful Death, which filled the house, held them united by his stiffened grasp." "Phoebe," Holgrave pleads, "Is it all terror?—nothing but terror? Are you conscious of no joy, as I am, that has made this the only point of life worth living for?"

Love permits a taste if not a measure of immortality: "It was in this hour, so full of doubt and awe, that the one miracle was wrought without which every human existence is a blank." Life *without* relationship is the blank in existence. Humanity must make what it can of its moment even as it struggles with itself. The enemy at this level, the killer of relationship, death, "the only guest who is certain, at one time or another, to find his way into every human dwelling," first appears in the opening pages of the novel, and it can be contextualized by those who have made life worthy. Humanized through relationship as "the guest," death serves the living through our acceptance of it.

Of course, a death can bring either good or bad fortune to others, and Hawthorne makes the distance between a matter of chance rather than virtue. The accidental death of an uncle in the previous generation has imprisoned the innocent Clifford, even as Jaffrey's own death could raise new murder charges against Clifford and against Hepzibah as well. Their escape is, in fact, a near thing.

When Clifford and Hepzibah panic and flee, leaving the dead Jaffrey in their house, they become suspects, and Hawthorne does everything he can to increase their peril. During their absence, the life of the street turns against them. Even before the body of Jaffrey is discovered, neighbors call for the city marshal against "the bloody brother" "at his old tricks" with "that awful-tempered Old Maid."

Critics explain the anger of the street as the world of commerce against the house of contemplation, but those in the house are not thoughtful. What they are is "old." They belong to the discarded and easily shunned past. In the chapter "Alice's Posies," by way of contrast, the always contemporary street is ageless, drawing from all cohorts, and each member of it, from the smallest child to the oldest habitué, assumes the worst of Clifford and Hepzibah. An urchin screams the common accusation as Phoebe returns. "There's something wicked there!" he shouts. "Don't—don't—don't go in!"

By increasing the vulnerability of Clifford and Hepzibah, Hawthorne claims that luck more than logic saves them from the circumstantial case building around them. Holgrave's daguerreotypes of the dead judge, the return of the suspects before public discovery of the body, and the innocence of Phoebe push "something wicked" into the commonplace of disease. When it is determined that Jaffrey has died of natural causes, "the public, with its customary alacrity, proceeded to forget that he had ever lived."

But can we forget the grasping materialism and betrayal that Jaffrey symbolizes? Hawthorne insists on the dark against the light and even admits to his editor that the book "darkens damnably toward the close," while adding, "I shall try hard to pour some setting sunshine over it." "Life is made up of marble and mud," he reports in "The Little Shop-Window." The keeper of these distinctions and ambivalences is the character Holgrave, the daguerreotypist who makes dark pictures out of sunlight. As Hawthorne's thinker, Holgrave bridges the generations and the distance between house and street, but at a cost. Early on, he is a radical theorist with "lack of reverence for what was fixed"; in the end, he welcomes "the impression of permanence."

Hawthorne predicts this change in a way that makes us respect the earlier man who lives alone more than his socially engaged reincarnation. "At almost every step of life," he observes in "The Daguerreotypist," "we meet with young men of just about Holgrave's age, for whom we anticipate wonderful things, but of whom, even after much and careful inquiry, we never happen to hear another word." This explanation ends in cruelty. "Like certain chintzes, calicoes, and ginghams, they show finely in their first newness, but cannot stand the sun and rain, and assume a very sober aspect after washing-day."

Why do we expect so much more of Holgrave than we receive? Why does Hawthorne make his most thoughtful character less thoughtful in the end? In "The Flower of Eden," Holgrave plans his future this way: "I have a presentiment, that, hereafter, it will be my lot to set out trees, to make fences—perhaps, even, in due time, to build a house for another generation—in a word, to conform myself to laws, and the peaceful practice of society." Must mature happiness sound so bland?

Conforming oneself to laws and the peaceful practice of society is surely what we expect in a grownup, and yet this slightly older person seems to be less creative and intense than the earlier youth who broods over the betrayal of his family and writes about it. The solitary thinker is less apparent in this newly settled family man couched in "the peaceful practice of society." Is that just the way it must be, or has compulsive absorption in the assignment of revenge used him up in some fundamental way?

Francis Bacon in "On Revenge" calls it "a kind of wild justice," and its completion in Holgrave appears to have tamed him intellectually. Bacon explains, "A man that studieth revenge, keeps his own wounds green." Holgrave has accepted definition from those wounds. We last find him with "a half-melancholy laugh," explaining just how much the betrayal of his line and the requirement that he answer it have consumed him. The means of belittling the Pyncheons, he reveals, "is the only inheritance that has come down to me from my ancestors." A poor legacy indeed. It seems to have left Holgrave somehow alone in the midst of Hawthorne's arranged happiness and prosperity.

3

LOUISA MAY ALCOTT MEETS MARK TWAIN
OVER THE YOUNG FACE OF CHANGE

Not for nothing have Washington Irving and Nathaniel Hawthorne made radical change a background theme in American fiction. Again and again, characters in early American fiction are bewildered by the alterations around them in an unstable present. Anxieties over what was happening were inevitable in a country driven so constantly by uncontrolled development. Perhaps it was just as inevitable that the novel of the developing child—as opposed to children's fiction—would parallel this phenomenon and become a focal point in dealing with uncertainties and apprehensions over change.

Nineteenth-century portrayals of children reflect both the hopes and fears of the nation. How will the growing child, symbol of an unknown future, handle a world moving out from under everyone? Will it do well, and on whose terms? Will it grow up straight or crooked, and depending on that moral divide, what will it do to America? Where will the child's sympathies come to rest? Will the coming adult maintain loyalty to the receding past, discard it with casual contempt, or simply forget it?

The two most renowned children in American literature are Josephine March and Huckleberry Finn. It is telling that they both appear in the second half of the nineteenth century, and they present opposing answers to the questions just raised. They are also in their time the fictional overseers of a new genre. A different kind of child protagonist enters American literature in the decades after the Civil War as the witness for what the nation stands for and what it does not. Whether boy or girl, this persona is equally the product and the critic of its civilization, and a last question—Of what use has the domestic scene been to the child's development?—is a vexed one.

Of course, any comparison of *Little Women* (1868–69) and *Adventures of Huckleberry Finn* (1885) runs risks. The first novel is a domestic romance about the intricacies in family life; the second is a social satire of a vagabond forced into flight. The books target very different audiences. Girls follow Louisa May Alcott's Jo March avidly. Boys dream of Huckleberry Finn. Alcott holds her readers with sentimentality—"moral pap for the young," as she called it in the cynical privacy of her journal. Mark

Twain relies on dialect, humor, and understatement. Slang is vulgar in Alcott's story; the soul of wit in Twain's. Conversation finds loving intimates in Alcott; it separates them as strangers in Twain. Alcott favors fireside tableaux; Twain loves antic display in the great outdoors.

Thematic contradictions naturally follow. The protagonists in *Little Women* correct themselves through the admonitions of their elders. They tell the truth. Guidance from the adult world controls their development. All alone and liking it that way, Huck distrusts adults and with good reason; many of them are trying to do him in. He survives in the world by feeling his way and telling lies. When tempted to be honest with Mary Jane Wilks, he explains, "A body that ups and tells the truth when he is in a tight place, is taking considerable many resks; though I ain't had no experience."

A reader who loves both stories is rare indeed. All the same, *Little Women* and *Huckleberry Finn* succeed as companion works. They share affinities that go unnoticed in the development of postbellum American fiction. As the best sellers of their time, they call upon the same expanding market. Both novels are about and for the young while keeping adult readers engaged, and each turns on a modern understanding of maturation with the growing concerns that child rearing comes to entail.

Alcott and Twain are the first American authors to capitalize fully on a child-centered culture of nurturance. They place that newly exalted status and its perceived vulnerabilities in creative tension with each other. From one side, they ask readers to enter a fictive world of child wish fulfillment. From the other side, they test the wherewithal of children who must stand for much more than childhood, and as often as not, this test comes over the subject's behavior in the presence of death.

It was not always thus. Children in earlier periods joined the workforce as soon as they were able, and death came too frequently for a writer to make it a new stage of awareness in the young person who witnessed it. Change from such matter-of-fact attitudes came gradually, but by the late 1860s, against the colossal bloodletting of the Civil War, greater recognition of human frailty made "tender youth" a popular subject, susceptibility its theme, and intimacy with loss a special source of concern.

Little Women and *Huckleberry Finn* owe much of their creativity and popularity to an incomplete moment in this transition. If the susceptibility of youth provided literary scope, it did not yet extend to the entitlements enjoyed by childhood a century and more later. Religious belief in innate corruption and one's fallen nature still cut across the privilege of youth. Concern for the soul overrode physical development, and the need for correction remained central to nineteenth-century child rearing.

These ramifications explain why such different characters as Jo March and Huck Finn can be obsessed by the same problem: their own conceived depravity. "How could I be so wicked?" cries Jo when her anger and indifference allow sister Amy to fall through the ice during a childhood adventure. "All right, then, I'll *go* to hell," answers Huck for not turning in the runaway slave Jim.

No reader ever bothers to believe in the accuracy of these pangs of guilt. We never question the innate goodness of Huck or the March sisters (Meg, Jo, Beth, and Amy). Why should we? And yet mystery as well as narrative tension remain over the presumed nature of goodness in these characters. What is the source of virtue in these worthy children? Where does it come from?

Neither author provides meaningful answers to these questions. An already apparent goodness generates interest in story. It is, to be sure, possible to lose "goodness," or to become "bad," and drama often centers on this point. Readers soon learn that a single lapse could mean disaster. As Jo exclaims in the chapter "Jo Meets Apollyon," "I'm afraid I *shall* do something dreadful some day, and spoil my life."

If this seems strange, we should remember that the literary authority in both novels is not only a religious work but the same book: John Bunyan's *The Pilgrim's Progress,* with Christian journeying toward heaven while hell lurks just a slip away. An allegory of conversion, *Pilgrim's Progress* is a frequent presence in *Little Women.* Huck, alone in the Grangerford library, reads "considerable in it now and then." Bunyan's book of correction functions as the crossover text for a mixed audience. It is the adult's guide for upbringing and a young reader's

standard to be met in the course of development. Not
incidentally, *Pilgrim's Progress* is about leaving home to
construct a better one, figuratively expressed as a heav-
enly one.

Leaving home plays a corresponding role in these
postbellum novels, but the conversion involved is determinedly social rather than religious in form. The mostly
absent father of the Marches may be a pastor, but he has
no visible congregation, and the girls appear in no regular church scene. Spiritual well-being is a given rather
than a practice. Huck, for his part, may fear hell, but he
lives in this world. Salvation is a secular journey in both
books, and the task of the young is to acknowledge its
implications. The March sisters and Huck attract readers because they cope with temporal problems.

The main conflicts in both novels take material form,
and it is significant that Alcott and Twain place their
protagonists on the downside of communal prosperity.
Diminished economic status means that their fictional
children must struggle to prove personal worth against
dominant forces of wealth, security, and power. Society
is ranged against the child, and the weight of that op-
position is great.

Narrative tension depends on the fact that the child
must deal with these economic conflicts at a disadvan-
tage, and the obtuse behavior of well-off adults raises an
important question. Is American civilization contribut-
ing to the child's welfare and goodness or standing in its
way? Here again the earlier and more fundamental ques-

tion is never answered: Where does "goodness" come from?

Poverty in both stories provides one of several tests of goodness. It allows arbitrary adults to intrude in harmful or misguided ways, and it tempts the young to act immorally. Each successful child must therefore learn to manipulate an acquisitive world to its advantage without stepping over a certain ethical line.

Continuing virtue in this struggle remains an obligation, but it means little if not in tandem with growing competence. Mistakes can be made, and plot needs rely on them, but no mistake must touch the integrity of the child. Here is the puzzle in both books. Neither Alcott nor Twain thinks that morality leads to success or even security as the world understands it, but the good child must never forget it. The children in these books charm us by being good; they succeed by knowing how to do something.

Tribulations—defeat, antagonism, betrayal, humiliation, loss, and death—fill the novels, and they touch the young with special vehemence. Perhaps the greatest assumption that Alcott and Twain share comes on this level. They agree that their children are always more interesting than the collection of adults around them. Adulthood possesses few charms, and the knowing child avoids maturation as long as possible.

Youth is essentially a gift, a better state than humdrum middle age or being old. In *Little Women* and *Huckleberry Finn,* adults occupy inert terrain and represent matter-of-fact reality. Mistakes in the young involve learning. Comparable mistakes in elders reveal a flaw in character. Ignorance in the child fuels humor; it exposes the foolish adult. The dynamic is everywhere in both novels with an underlying purpose. What reader would not identify more with the child in this contrast over the stages of life?

A deeper question turns on the meaning of adulthood as seen through the mysterious trajectory of the child. What will the process of unavoidable change come to mean? Alcott has the March sisters grow up, while Twain leaves Huck in permanent boyhood, and it is this difference that makes a comparison of *Little Women* and *Huckleberry Finn* useful for present purposes. Alcott makes careful use of change; Twain arrests it. Nonetheless, both situations open into the challenge of being alone.

The two story lines, acceptance and evasion of adulthood, bracket one of the deepest worries in nineteenth-century American understandings of maturity. Virtue in the youthful protagonist must contend with negative experience in the world. That is a given, and it raises a troubling issue. Can one be absolutely good and succeed, or must the child make a compromise with something unpleasant in reality to succeed? Moreover, if compromise is necessary, when and how should innocence be qualified?

The explanation given for lack of prosperity in the March family is noteworthy in this regard. In "Gossip," the opening chapter of volume two, we learn that Mr.

March "has the strict integrity which shut him out from the more worldly successes." Huck's world, in turn, is completely dominated by acquisitive people, but Twain protects his permanent boy from their influence and this vice.

As different as they are, Alcott and Twain also give similar answers to the unlikely prospect of innocent success. Each implies that the idealism of youth will founder more than a little in adult life. Thus, Meg's "home-love" struggles to recover its energy during marriage when naiveté trips her up in "On the Shelf." Huck's disgust when town loafers in Brickville pour turpentine on a stray dog and set it on fire for their amusement is ours, but it can take passive form only in a child.

The strain between childish conception and the need for competent action in a crisis is the dramatic fulcrum that drives both books. At stake is how and where reality will intrude and be met. We worry about Meg's inexperience in marriage when she is caught in the drudgeries of homemaking. Conversely, although a child cannot intrude, we expect Huck would do more for the dog in Brickville as an adult. Twain is careful to have Huck work behind the scenes at times to make a right result prevail.

Fictions about childhood use this quality of difference as a form of anticipation. What will the child become? Alcott and Twain take opposite tacks to the coming problem of maturity, but they keep us reading the same way; they dangle the partially known prospect of the adult in the child's thought. Buried in this theme is a similar question about the growing pains of a nation that still likes to think of itself as young.

Whether as tentative adult or permanent child, only the young person seriously reflects about its situation in these books, and this trait secures our hope for them. We admire Meg for beginning the uncertain adjustment out of her secure childhood. Huck, without that security, is an escape artist, but the tonal accuracies in his voice save him; they tell us that something beyond a boy's spirit stands in the way of the cruelty he sees all around him. The goodness of the young person implies virtue retained in the republican experiment. But for how long?

Little Women

No longer just a story for young girls, though it is still that, Alcott's novel reads now as a canonical work for both sexes and all ages. In *Revolution from Within* (1992), Gloria Steinem announces the critical shift. "Where else . . . could we have read about an all-female group who discussed work, art, and all the Great Questions, or found girls who wanted to be women and not vice versa?" *Little Women* shows the path to becoming a successful adult. Despite a mawkish plot, Alcott looks hard at what it takes to grow up well.

Immature behavior can be found in these pages, but it is never encouraged. In "Castles in the Air," midway through volume one, the juvenile aspirations of the March sisters receive titular comeuppance even before the girls deliver them. Each child asks for a success that is unrealistic. Meg seeks marriage for love but with "nice food, pretty clothes, handsome furniture, pleasant people, and heaps of money." Jo's books will make her "rich and famous." Amy will become "the best artist in the whole world." Beth, third youngest, bespeaks a different but equally powerful impulse. She wants "to stay at home safe with father and mother" in the hope that nothing will ever change.

The lofty nature of the ambitions in three of the sisters and the impracticality of the failing fourth, not the basic desires themselves, are at fault. Remember, as well, that all except Beth's dream require money to achieve their ends. Jo reasons for all of them in "A Friend." "She saw that money conferred power; money and power, therefore, she resolved to have." As Alcott wryly adds, "The purpose which now took possession of her was a natural one to a poor and ambitious girl."

The second volume of *Little Women* squelches an aspect in each dream. Meg marries for love but to a poor man and struggles to raise children in drab conditions. Although Jo sells stories, she ends up running a school for boys with an unlikely husband, the rather pedantic and much older Professor Bhaer. Beth, who wants only to be with her parents, gets her wish in a lethal twist. She dies at home as what she is, a child in arrested development. Amy, the only sister to marry wealth, becomes an art patron when she realizes that she lacks the talent to be creative on her own.

The point of Alcott's exercise in diminished returns is twofold. At one level, each sister achieves partial fulfillment of her plan, with something withheld. Even Beth achieves ironic success in "Beth's Secret": "I have a feeling that it never was intended I should live long," she confides in Jo. "I never made any plans about what I'd do when I grew up." For Alcott, the adventure in childhood requires adjustment to change. Beth is unable to adjust to experience and does not want to change. In response, readers never identify with Beth as they do with each of her sisters.

At a second level of implication, Alcott's exercises in growing up deliver a gendered message to all women. For while love and marriage remain keys for all three March sisters who reach adulthood, Alcott insists that marriage cannot be the goal in life. Jo seems destined for the appealing neighborhood boy, Laurie, who declares his love early on, but Alcott, in her dismissal of all castles in the air, will have none of it. Jo is made to reject Laurie. Marriage might be in the cards, but it can never be enough in itself.

Tough-minded Alcott, the opposite of her sentimental narrator, is as amusing as she is instructive on this score. "Publishers won't let authors finish up as they like but insist on having people married off in a wholesale manner," she writes to her friend Elizabeth Powell. "'Jo' should have remained a literary spinster, but so many enthusiastic young ladies wrote to me clamorously demanding that she should marry Laurie, or somebody, that I didn't dare to refuse & out of perversity went & made a funny match for her. I expect vials of wrath to be poured upon my head, but rather enjoy the prospect."

More than humor or even gender lies behind Alcott's unromantic decision. Critiques of children's literature often trivialize its deeper registers, but any book that holds audiences across time must have a vital philosophical dimension of conflict somewhere in the mix of it. Alcott, in poor health and the provider for her family, including her sisters and parents, knew the struggle of life. She wants the readers of *Little Women* to see that struggle, and her most interesting device comes through the figure that no one can relate to, "stupid little Beth"; the name carefully rhymes with death.

Maturity in *Little Women* comes not in marriage but through the knowledge of loss. Beth's final illness and death redefine her closest sister and the book's protagonist, Jo. Mr. March, modeled on Bronson Alcott, Louisa's ethereal father, gets things only half right when he notes of his brashest daughter, "She doesn't bounce, but moves quietly, and takes care of a certain little person in a motherly way." This thought, in a chapter coyly entitled "Pleasant Meadows," misses the growth in Jo. Much more is at stake than a "wild girl" turning into "a strong, helpful, tender-hearted woman."

Alcott makes Beth pay the price for refusing to grow up, but her death serves a critical function. Beth embodies the need in knowing how to die well, a lesson for all families amidst the high mortality rates of children in the nineteenth century. It was a rare grouping of any size that did not suffer child death in the home. Alcott taps into this common experience to exhibit Jo's maturation. "God seems so far away I can't find him," Jo reveals in "Dark Days" as Beth weakens. The primary caretaker, Jo sees how cruel existence can be, and yet death itself brings new direction.

Four lessons from Beth's death reveal Jo to be a serious thinker in a chapter aptly named "All Alone." The first lesson comes, as it often does, from Alcott's title to the chapter. Against fatality we *are* alone, and must call upon inner strength to bear it, as Beth manages to do arranging the good death in her own way. Second, and related to the first lesson, Jo recognizes that death breaks even the closest unit. The family has been the best thing for Jo the child; now, because the March family is less, it no longer encompasses. "Everyone seems going away from me," Jo reflects to herself, "and now I am all alone." The home remains, but the domestic scene at the center of the novel is gone. Although that scene gave Jo the comfort zone for thought that she needed, she now learns to think harder without it.

Solitude, the state required for reflection, provides the third lesson. It encourages Jo to be herself in the stories she wants to tell. Until this point she has churned out pulp fiction for the magazines. Now, writing from "the heart" and "with no thought of fame or money," she has, in her father's words, "found your style at last." But as the fourth lesson in "All Alone" conveys, Father March is again only half right. Jo, like Alcott, writes from the head as well as the heart. She has developed an adult perspective with her own view of the world. Instead of the family defining her, it has become her subject.

Jo turns to her father, a rare occurrence, for the fourth lesson of "All Alone," and she discovers that her parent, even as a minister, has no more of an answer than she over the loss of Beth. They converse in the study named "the church of one member," a significant break from Alcott's gestures of familial cohesion. To resolve "the want of faith that made life look so dark" requires reflection. Jo learns that life must be managed through careful thought. This is the moment she grows up.

Alcott signals as much by seizing upon the scene: "The time had come when they could talk together not only as father and daughter, but as man and woman, able and glad to serve each other with mutual sympathy as well as mutual love." Death, the equalizer, brings Jo to her father's intellectual plane. In effect, the scene gives more: her growth against her father's static state carries her beyond him.

The proof of Jo's new ascendancy comes in the very next chapter, "Surprises," with Laurie's return as the husband of Amy. Laurie rushes in and expects to "go back to the happy old times," but Jo, alone among her peers, has dealt with death directly and intimately. "We never can be boy and girl again," she instantly reproves him; "the happy old times can't come back." "We are man and woman now," she adds, "with sober work to do, for play-time is over, and we must give up frolicking."

It is important to recognize what solitude has accomplished, even though Jo's state of being alone is of short duration. She has learned what she can be in her own eyes. She has decided to put away childish things, and is ready to assert herself in the world, which opens new vistas, though not without an undercurrent of loss. Jo on the threshold of adulthood speaks to us at this point more worthy of a reader's full respect, but she also somehow becomes of less interest in a book on childhood.

Why? The answer has as much to do with generic expectations as it does with recognition of change. The child protagonist is a figure of wish fulfillment that a reader lets go of slowly and grudgingly. Such a figure holds back the forces of change. Like the nation itself, Jo is most attractive as imagination and promise. Reality is the commonplace in the quotidian of daily practice; it can never be as grand.

Another and more convenient demise gives Jo's growth direction. As so often in fiction, so in the final chapter of *Little Women,* death gives even as it takes away. Elderly Aunt March, an unpleasant censor of her poor relations and "the terror of all boys for miles around," has left her estate to Jo, who turns it into a school for wayward boys with her husband. The new Mrs. Bhaer, thwarted earlier as Jo by her rich aunt's caprice, wonders with satisfaction "how poor, dear Aunt March would have lamented had she been there to see the sacred precincts of prim, well-ordered Plumfield overrun with Toms, Dicks, and Harrys."

Alcott buys into a pattern in American literature with this ending. Her final chapter, aptly entitled "Harvest Time," displays a new generation reaping what a previous one would have misunderstood and abhorred in a changing world. Jo's triumph does not mean an easy life, never an option in Alcott. No longer a writer but a caretaker of the children her husband teaches, she pauses to recount the blemishes in a circumstance of constant toil, but she has to admit to herself "I'm far happier than I deserve."

These final remarks feed a level in existence that is also wisdom, what Jo herself terms "unromantic facts." They reach beyond castles in the air and even beyond the tensions in Alcott's fiction. Jo, who has always complained about something, now decides "I have nothing to complain of." Happiness in the mature adult, it turns out, is a managed state rather than a dreamed-of condition.

Adventures of Huckleberry Finn

No matter how much we identify with Huck, we never get the level of intimacy we achieve with Jo March, and the difference is instructive. Something about Huck is unknowable and withheld. All the same, we have to worry about him even though he overcomes every difficulty with aplomb. We worry because Huck's troubles would overwhelm anyone else, whether child or adult.

Without mother or home, Huck has been beaten, imprisoned, and nearly murdered by his alcoholic father. He is despised and feared by his community, misunderstood, challenged, and misled by anyone who tries to help, abused by a series of confidence men, threatened or dismissed by almost every adult he meets on the Mississippi River, and exposed to more than thirty deaths, including that of his father.

Huck nearly drowns, sees murders, watches a lynch mob, barely escapes a disastrous blood feud, and narrowly survives other desperate situations, while simultaneously violating the deepest convictions and the law of his culture. Where does his incredible fortitude come from? In a 1953 issue of the *Listener,* the poet W. H. Auden asks a reasonable question: Why isn't this "small child" a "trembling nervous wreck"?

The answer is that Huck is no ordinary child, or for that matter, an ordinary American, despite all the attempts to make him represent his country. Neither fish nor fowl in this regard, he is a fanciful combination of both, a mixed creature of nostalgia and wish fulfillment. Huck succeeds as Twain's "American Boy," and we cannot see him without knowing what this designation means.

"Personal familiarity" is the only virtue Twain claims for himself as he introduces the lost slave culture of his childhood from the 1840s, a vicious world that serves larger purposes precisely because it both horrified and enthralled the writer. *Adventures of Huckleberry Finn* records the full force of malice in the town life of the antebellum South against the very few decent people who help a young boy on the run. Huck is Twain's rhetorical device as much as his subject in making a little good overcome a lot of bad, but it is not an easy task, and to manage it, Twain divides Huck into usable parts.

We first encounter Huck in chapter six of *The Adventures of Tom Sawyer* (1876), where, as "the juvenile pariah of the village," a boy of twelve, he is "idle and lawless and vulgar and bad." Only the first of these qualities, idleness, describes Huck in either novel, and it is an excusable trait in a child. The string of accusations comes from the wrongheaded elders of the town. Twain's fictional St. Petersburg, placed in Missouri, is the home of homeless Huck; he is half of, half not of St. Petersburg. In Puritan vernacular, he is in but not of the world, and the stance makes him a touchstone of cultural ills.

Huck's divided quality is foreshadowed in this first novel of adolescent adventure. *Tom Sawyer* ends with the warning that it is "strictly a history of a *boy*" and "must stop" because, as Twain explains, "the story could not go much further without becoming the history of a *man*." Man and boy occupy separate worlds with different codes of behavior in Twain's fiction, and the distinction assigns intrinsic worth to permanent boyhood. Even so, Huck remains usefully double. He fluctuates somewhere between child and youth based on the emotional dictates of each narrative moment.

Twain's sliding scale explains his understanding of the American Boy, a designation carefully distinguished from "Model Boy," the mocking epithet applied to Tom Sawyer's insufferable younger brother, Sid. Twain insists on the distinction, but like Alcott, he never explains the origins of "good" child against "bad" child. It is enough to show how the two kinds of boy operate when given the chance.

The American Boy is naughty but dependable within the code of conduct of his peers. The Model Boy is a hypocrite geared to elders. He plays the adult system for advantage by confusing the codes of boy and adult. Sid Sawyer, and others like him, trick the adult world by appearing falsely "good." A projection of adult standards, they are hardly real boys at all in Twain's conception. They are "models" that the adult world encourages by ignoring the true nature of the child.

Meanwhile, Twain's stark separation of boy from man gives Huck an escape hatch and secures his integrity. He is the real boy—sometimes a child, sometimes more of an adolescent—but steady in his assigned role. Twain's very title—not *Huckleberry Finn* but *Adventures of Huckleberry Finn*—underwrites this claim of consistency. Seemingly older or seemingly younger, Huck presides at the same tonal level in every unfolding scene of the novel. He is the partially knowing narrator of Twain's satire in picaresque form.

The novel gives adventure after passing adventure in even sequence, with Huck remaining the same throughout. Like Don Quixote in Cervantes's version of the genre, Huck is the unwavering picaro who half witnesses and half endures the foibles of his culture. Huck functions as the reliable spectator in every situation, and that reliability allows us to trust him even when he doesn't recognize the situation for what it is. Humor takes over when our own understanding replaces the boy's limited but sincere knowledge.

Boyhood, so defined, secures Huck's innate goodness. Every reader quickly accepts what the world of the novel denies. This goodness is never explained, but we recognize it through related characteristics. The tenderness of youth permits Huck to leave the deadpan delivery assigned to him when Twain needs more emotion, and this same tenderness helps to separate Huck from the cruelty he witnesses, allowing Twain to inoculate the designated boy from the mean-spiritedness all around him. Huck knows society is against him, and it teaches him to do his own thinking.

The first quality, a boy's compassion for those in trouble, has no bounds; it applies to friend and foe alike and is ecumenical in spirit. As he watches the slaughter of friends in the Grangerford-Shepherdson feud, he reports "it made me so sick I most fell out of the tree," a natural reaction, and yet the same words—"it made me sick to see it"—apply just as well to the tarring and feathering of the despicable Duke and King, the confidence men who make life on the raft miserable.

Tenderness of heart encourages Huck to document wrong on all sides of every issue without the slightest hint of self-righteousness. The Duke and the King deserve punishment for their swindling ways, but how much punishment and what kind? Huck is properly horrified by the enraged mob's brutal treatment of them. "Human beings *can* be awful cruel to one another," he exclaims. Earlier, when the Duke and the King dupe the innocent, he can be just as judgmental from the other side without losing integrity: "It was enough to make a body ashamed of the human race."

If there is a problem in watching from the sidelines, boyhood minimizes it. Huck decries the evil he sees everywhere, but nothing in him suggests any hope of an answer to it. Twain is pessimistic about human nature and demands this limitation in his protagonist. He has made Huck a credible witness rather than a corrector of behavior, a decision that coincides with his understanding of the boy as permanent child.

The second quality in Huck's goodness, his isolation, deserves more attention. Shunned by the town of St. Petersburg and homeless, Huck turns separation into a virtue. Unlike others in his world, Huck enjoys being alone, knows the meaning of solitude, and uses both to get past the prejudice of his community. Here he is in "I Spare Miss Watson's Jim":

> By and by it got sort of lonesome, and so I went and set on the bank and listened to the currents washing along, and counted the stars and drift-logs and rafts that come down, and then went to bed; there ain't no better way to put in time when you are lonesome; you can't stay so, you soon get over it.

We never worry about Huck when he is alone; he is clearly safest that way, and the opportunity always stimulates thought. "You Can't Pray a Lie" gives Huck struggling with himself "to see if I couldn't try to quit being the kind of boy I was and be better." Here Huck confronts the idea of the "Model Boy" that a corrupt society values. To turn Jim in as a runaway would be the town's way to become "better." Only the outcast can reach an opposite conclusion and "go to hell" for Jim.

Twain illustrates the American Boy to perfection in this scene. "I studied a minute, sort of holding my breath," Huck notes, deciding "forever, betwixt two things." The thoughts that save Jim correspond to the boy's view of the society that enslaves Jim in the first place. Treating Jim as a slave *for* the town runs against the comfort zone of the boy's separate code. It means "my heart warn't right," "I warn't square," "I was playing double." The integrity in the code of the boy is familiar, that of adult society is not. Acknowledged naughtiness, well short of actual malice, is the key here. "I would take up wickedness again," Huck reasons, "which was in my line, being brung up to it."

The question remains, though. How can this American Boy be so precocious in thought beyond the understanding of his society? How can he be so good without the tutelage and nurture of a home? Naughtiness carries us only so far in getting Huck to another plane of racial understanding that his culture will not even begin to achieve without another decade and a half of political strife and four years of civil war.

Simply put, this boy is no boy at all but a forty-nine-year-old southerner living in the North four decades into the future and imagining the adolescent he would have liked to be but never was. Dripping with nostalgia, Twain's rendition of boyhood is a saga of the way we never could have been. Negative and positive impulses compete in Twain's daydream of childhood's return, and both celebrate escapism from it all. We have escape *from* the father, escape *with* a subordinate, escape *against* regimentation, and, above all, escape *away* from the inanity of social life—what Huck sitting uncomfortably but quietly at the Wilks dinner table describes as "humbug talky-talk, just the way people always does."

Twain's escapist plot means that Huck can do what people never get to do but would like to try. Who has not imagined life as an independent child who has the competence, the ability, and the emotional control to outwit every adult who stands in the way? Of course, the negatives in escapism give us something else: beneath the vernacular and humor, we have a lost and homeless boy with nowhere to go. Huck can remain so calmly the same because he represents a world that is as static in conception as it is lost to history.

Twain's nostalgia over this vanished world also explains why he wants Huck to be alone. The boy who puzzles through the cruelty of town life alongside the natural beauty of life on the Mississippi in the 1840s can indulge a vision of the past that no one would want to repeat through practical engagement. Not for the last time, solitude is a defense mechanism in a world that does not deserve to be saved.

One must therefore be careful in the uses and directions of solitude. Huck, like Twain, has a morbid streak, which is a danger in prolonged isolation. In a gratuitous aside, one without ulterior purpose, Huck reflects in free-wheeling style when he arrives at the Phelps plantation near the end of the novel:

> When I got there it was all still and Sunday-like, and hot and sunshiny; the hands was gone to the fields; and there was them kind of faint dronings of bugs and flies in the air that makes it seem so lonesome and like everybody's dead and gone; and if a breeze fans along and quivers the leaves it makes you feel mournful, because you feel like it's spirits whispering—spirits

> that's been dead ever so many years—and you
> always think they're talking about *you*. As a
> general thing it makes a body wish *he* was dead,
> too, and done with it all.

Huck disappears in world weariness and a desire to be "done with it all" in this passage. We move from a first-person point of view ("I got there"), to indirect second-person address ("you feel mournful"), to an objectified third-person claim ("makes a body wish *he* was dead") as a slow Sunday afternoon rolls into cycles of eternity. Too much time alone twists identity instead of strengthening it.

Critics use passages like this one to call Huck a death-haunted boy, and they base their claims on more than the fact that he sees so much of it. Huck kills off a dozen imaginary families in the lies that he tells to friend and foe alike—to Judith Loftus and the Grangerfords, on the side of virtue, to the slave-catchers as well as the Duke and the King, on the side of vice, and on and on. But if Huck is death haunted, it does not define or change him. He has no intimacy with death in the way that Jo March experiences it, and the difference allows him to remain a boy, while Jo turns into an adult.

The constantly moving figure on the raft never establishes enough of a relationship to grieve for anyone except the escaping slave, Jim, who is deliberately saved time and again as Huck's one touch point of stability.

Huck escapes even the death of his father through the filtered and retrospective account of this one adult protector, Jim, and the news brings relief rather than sorrow. Huck sees death all around him, but the child in him remains untouched by its meaning. Death is everywhere at one level, but it exists only within the picaresque surfaces of Twain's constantly moving story.

If many readers remain fascinated by the boy Huck more than the grown woman Mrs. Josephine M. Bhaer, out of the girl Jo, it is because childhood holds the imagination in the novel of the child. We fully grasp Jo March because she grows up and explains herself even as she forgets some of what it meant to be a child. She has conquered childhood at the proper moment. Huck never grows up and resists us through the difference. His voice welcomes us, but the speaker of the words slips away from us just as inevitably as our own childhood has disappeared into a shadowy past.

When Huck in the end decides "to light out for the territory ahead of the rest," he sustains the mystery of childhood in an imaginary America, and his elusiveness translates into further hopes of escape—escape, not least, from all the changes that are destroying the America he knows. Permanent boyhood holds to the past. Huck reacts against the world that is coming into being, and his plan of escape retains logical power as long as he is alone on the run and away from the social pressures that come to every adult. We identify with this plan without being able to live it.

Jo does not light out. "Glancing from her husband to her children, tumbling on the grass beside her," she worries about her husband's age ("Fritz is getting gray and stout"), her own health ("I'm growing as thin as a shadow"), the behavior of children ("that incorrigible Tommy"), financial security ("we never shall be rich"), and the safety of her home ("Plumfield may burn up any night"). These are the anxieties of every parent struggling to make do for others in an insecure world.

That said, the banal worries of the family woman in *Little Women* are just as deliberate, just as conclusive, and just as moving in their own way as Huck's last magical words in *Adventures of Huckleberry Finn.* One wonders if Jo might not be similarly alone or as threatened in her anxious thoughts as Huck in his alienation from society. Far from the aspiration of an imagined America that Huck represents, Jo grapples with the concrete, enmeshed, exhausting aspects of its daily reality.

The motto of the United States, e pluribus unum, conjures up a hidden corollary: mutatis mutandis; and the two together contain the hopes and fears of the unfolding nation in competing theories of change. Will the inevitability of "things being changed that have to be changed" encourage or hinder the ongoing national process of "from many one"? Does change drive Americans apart or bring them together? It is the rare public figure who lives long enough who does not also give way to despair over the course of the republic. That is why hope and despair flit back and forth across the pages of both novels.

There is therefore a last similarity in these different books about the American child. Just as Huck resists change, so Jo comes to fear it as an adult. How many Americans dealing with flux all around them wish for things to remain as they are and want to resist what comes next? Public discourse in American politics turns constantly on this tension. Do we advance, or do we try to remain the same? Still popular today, *Little Women* and *Adventures of Huckleberry Finn* thrive on the same anxiety by giving more of an answer. The dramatically engaged child against mundane adulthood allows us to stand still for a moment—a strategy we can accept as a welcome fantasy only because we always expect the real child to grow up and would think it a tragedy if it did not.

4

HENRY JAMES AND ZORA NEALE HURSTON ANSWER DEFEAT

Defeat is specific, and we remember it longer than triumph. The world summarizes it by saying "we learn through sad experience," but like most truisms, this one hides a vital ingredient. The real teacher is not sad experience. The lesson learned, if learned at all, comes through acceptance of one's own role. Only reassessment, a form of control when there is no other answer, restores the self to itself.

Defeat thus presents its own way of being alone. The disappointment and cost to identity in it summon the need for solitude, and we see as much in the novels to be taken up here, *The Portrait of a Lady* by Henry James in 1881 and *Their Eyes Were Watching God* by Zora Neale Hurston in 1937.

The protagonists in these stories, Isabel Archer and Janie Mae Crawford, are defeated by people close to them, and they must grow beyond the problem while still defined through it by others around them. The precise nature of defeat has to be known and digested for renewal to take place. Defeat and realization therefore go hand in hand in the genre of the bildungsroman, the novel of personal development and changed status.

Isabel and Janie first attract attention through their superficial qualities, the common plight of the beautiful woman, especially when alone. Made wonderful through the observations of others, both characters gradually see that appearances have ensnared them in understandings that are not their own. Social convention may be most insidious when it uses attraction as its barometer of meaning.

What does it mean to receive definition from outside of oneself? Often enough in American fiction, an attractive girl on the brink of womanhood symbolizes her civilization. On her arrival in England, Isabel Archer appears dressed "in the folds of the national banner." "The ear of the world is more directly presented" to her than to "sisters in other lands." Hurston introduces Janie Mae Crawford in similar terms. She represents "the world and the heavens boiled down to a drop."

Although these impossibly enlarged and imposed conceptions may flatter their subjects, they also tie them to the world's view of worth. They create portraits of ladies, but a portrait is necessarily fixed, and that is not all. A portrait is confined by the narrowness of a frame, and it implies refinement more than growth.

Despite their differences, the novels present similar ideas about how growth beyond such appearances can occur. Isabel and Janie go forward as the smartest of characters, but that is not enough, even though we accept in them an acuity that the world of story ignores. Independent thought, the key to new development, happens only in defeat. Each woman finds herself through the mistakes she makes—mistakes that seem obvious despite clear intelligence in the maker of them. These mistakes slowly grow into a sense of defeat beyond the maker's control, and the extent of the problem must first be gauged for what it is to regain control.

The tribulations of Isabel and Janie are invariably with men in ways that force them to cultivate an inner life. Their portraits, drawn by others, are male anticipations of the lady placed in a proper home. When that happens, and intimacy in the home turns into estrangement, the alienated self beyond the portrait has only itself to turn to. As for the men who want to lead them into those homes, something is always the matter with them in both James and Hurston. They are weak, ill, obtuse, demanding, grasping, selfish, brutal, vain, or morally devious. The more available the man to the woman in these novels, the more limited he becomes for a heroine defined by inner growth and outward adventure.

Neither Isabel nor Janie marries well, proving once again that marriage cannot define the intelligent woman.

What, then, *does* define her? James and Hurston find their answers in an accomplished point of view, no simple matter. Developing a point of view requires more than seeing well. The successful life demands tenacity as well as skill in dealing with a conniving world. In both stories the heroine is misled. Perception begins in the ability to live with the mistakes that follow misconception.

As such, *The Portrait of a Lady* and *Their Eyes Were Watching God* depict intellectual courage in feminine garb. James, in the later preface to his novel, reports he has written of "deep difficulty braved." Accuracy at "the window of perception" requires an act of will; a viewer can see what must be seen only by adjusting to a dilemma. Perception means "one seeing more where the other sees less, one seeing black where the other sees white, one seeing big where the other sees small, one seeing coarse where the other sees fine." Vision never stops with itself; it must wrestle with what others see and fail to see.

The Jamesian "spreading field" is the scene of deception, and Hurston's novel warns of the same difficulty. Seeing accurately when challenged or in trouble requires a knowledge of self against social pressure. An eligible widow in Eatonville, Janie answers by choosing exploration over the restrictive view assigned to her. "Everybody's . . . got tuh find out about livin' fuh theyselves," she says.

Not finding out for oneself is the tragedy that restricts further development. Difficulties enter in where to look, how to look, and what to take from it. It is no accident that the titles of both novels privilege what is seen. Whether followed or observed, the active life creates distortions in perception all around it, and when it is misunderstood, that life must resist the imposed anxieties that keep people from choosing an adventure that is growth.

Janie expresses the issue well. "It was all according to the way you see things," she reasons. "Some people could look at a mud-puddle and see an ocean with ships"; others settle for "scraps." Janie, like Isabel, will not accept the narrow view. When a hurricane brings death and destruction all around her in the Everglades of Florida, she has no regrets over the risk she is taking. "If you kin see de light at daybreak, you don't keer if you die at dusk," she explains. "It's so many people never seen de light at all."

Inevitably the problems in seeing are complicated for the beautiful woman by the fact that she is always "seen" first. She is approached and defined by her looks, not her intelligence or her interests. No one is given unlimited time to refine the self, and the young woman is pressed for lifelong decisions before she is fully formed or had the time to become wise. All too frequently, she is chosen instead of choosing. There may be no time for adjustments. Meaningful experience may come too late.

Henry James illustrates the value of negative experience during Isabel's first visit to Gardencourt, the English country home of the Touchetts. "The ghost" at Gardencourt "has never been seen by a young, happy,

innocent person," which defines Isabel at this point.
"You must have suffered first, have suffered greatly, have
gained some miserable knowledge," Ralph Touchett,
her cousin, tells her. Hurston refers in the same vein to
knowledge from "suffering without reason."

The twists and turns of life—when freighted with
pain, contention, injustice, or simple disappointment—
stop us in our tracks. Their residues are self-pity, resignation, bitterness, complaint, excuse, exhaustion—and
every one of these reactions is dangerous for the prospect of new growth.

The question asked by each author is the same. Will
new growth occur against the corruption of hope and
promise, or will the heroine retreat? Shorn of innocence
and stopped by social constraints, Isabel and Janie must
cope with the unacceptable terms imposed on them.
The sign of successful adulthood is not resignation or
even recognition but equanimity and continued thought
in the face of despair. A new mental composure sustains
each heroine, and we see them at the last poised for new
adventure.

Avoidance of risk is its own problem in the adventur-
ing heroine. Custom, vogue, routine, tradition, norms,
and usage are insidious snares for the developing
woman, and she must resist or at least contain them.
Conventional understanding unfairly imposed is the
ultimate enemy, with marriage and a home counting as
the main convention for a woman attractive to men.
Both novels give these pressures in excruciating detail.

Marriage is the negative source as well as the catalyst that forces new growth.

Hurston, writing much later, may even have had *The Portrait of a Lady* in mind. Marriage begins as a benevolent tyranny in both stories, and it soon moves to something much worse. Warned against the "awful chance" she is taking in marrying a third time, Janie accepts the risk by saying "no mo' than anybody else takes when dey gits married." Social mores, sexual restraints, and law "cover" the wife through her husband's control of property, the vow of obedience, and the unavailability of divorce.

The bad marriages of Isabel to Gilbert Osmond and of Janie to Jody Starks take similar form. Both husbands try to destroy the personalities of their wives by reducing them to objects on display. Isabel realizes that Osmond "would have liked her to have nothing of her own but her pretty appearance." "The real offence, as she ultimately perceived, was her having a mind of her own at all." Janie's situation is comparable. She reveals "ah'm stone dead from standing still and trying tuh smile."

That Isabel and Janie are beaten down into lonely "covered" women through marriage becomes clear from the imagery used to describe their situations. Isabel deliberately turns her own face into a mask, while Janie must wear a head-rag against her will. Both practices deny the woman's nature. Isabel's changeable eyes are her expressive trait; Janie's flowing hair, her most attractive feature.

Outsiders, mesmerized by the object on display, envy these beautiful wives who live in the finest of houses. Nevertheless, in images used of and by both women, they are prisoners in the marital house that is no home. The four walls suffocate them. Their husbands bind them to an arbitrary will—first, to prove authority, but then to conquer the inner person they have come to hate. The intrusiveness of this masculine insistence has no limits and accepts no answer. Isabel and Janie struggle against the same impossible choices. They must surrender all identity or face communal condemnation for refusing to comply.

But if Isabel and Janie appear trapped, spousal imposition has the opposite effect intended. In each case, resentment in the lonely and threatened wife leads to a secret life of thought, the place where an independent view can develop and thrive under the cloak of respectability. James and Hurston describe this inner life at great length and with larger purposes in mind. As Hurston writes of Janie, "She had an inside and an outside now and suddenly she knew how not to mix them."

Pillars in public understanding, Gilbert Osmond and Jody Starks are moral monsters who manipulate social norms in the home. They hide behind the precept that the good wife must obey her husband. Isabel and Janie struggle in silent frustration against these externally sanctioned manipulations, and while their efforts are fruitless within the marriage itself, they slowly liberate the individual. Through hidden thoughts passionately held, each wife acquires a resourcefulness previously lacking.

Isabel and Janie turn into intellectual rebels within their restricted situations. Pushed to the wall, they must decide where the limits in obedience lie, and to do so effectively they must turn the question. Creativity in thought often comes through learning the right question to ask. Held in place by "why must the wife always obey the husband?" the two women become independent thinkers by asking, "Who has the right to define disobedience?" To think this new way is to challenge propriety itself, and it requires a very different image of self beneath the public portrait of the lady.

Although actual revolt comes to each wife only when her personal integrity is openly violated by her husband, preparation for this act of courage has already freed her to answer husband and society on a new level. Isabel, so eager to be liked in the opening chapters of the novel, has overcome all such need by the end of it. She has found her own image rather than the portrait that exists for others. She will "never again feel a superficial embarrassment" over what people think or ask her to do or be.

Janie resists similar social pressures in Eatonville when, as a new widow alone, she hears "over and again" that "uh woman by herself is uh pitiful thing." Like Isabel, she moves within her discovered identity without regard for town opinion. Both women have learned how to live in comfort with themselves and by themselves.

The intellectual distance covered inwardly is the interest in both stories. James and Hurston have given us heroines capable of mental adventure across ideological boundaries but with a twist. Serious reflection begins in the home, moves beyond it, and then returns home in a new way. This sense of mental enclosure is especially important. The domestic scene is deliberately impoverished in these stories, but the space of the home exists *inside* the portrait, where the woman's thought can develop away from the external frame of the lady seen and assumed.

The domestic frame of reference, as opposed to the domestic scene, never disappears in either novel, despite the fact that Isabel and Janie live constantly on the move and hardly qualify as domestic figures. In the end, private and public settings merge in the one residential moment that always has a public dimension. As in *Little Women,* death in the home provides the final testing ground for Isabel and Janie. The dying Ralph Touchett prepares us for these possibilities in *The Portrait of a Lady,* but what he reveals reaches both novels. He is the Jamesian vehicle when he says, "There's nothing makes us feel so much alive as to see others die."

The Portrait of a Lady

No good partner exists for Isabel Archer, and Henry James is unusually direct in proving the absence of one. Of her three suitors, the likeliest possibility, Lord

Warburton, wears a white hat too large for him. He lives in "a wilderness of faded chintz" with two vacuous sisters, and he professes liberal views inconsistent with his privileges as an English aristocrat. The American businessman Caspar Goodwood is simple-minded physicality, as his name implies. He is unfinished and lacks "easy consonance with the deeper rhythms of life." Isabel's successful wooer, Gilbert Osmond, is "a sterile dilettante." He will "never, in the concert of pleasure, touch the big drum by so much as a knuckle."

Clearly there is no ideal partner in this grouping, but why does Isabel choose the worst of the lot, the one man that every valued acquaintance rejects as wrong for her? Mrs. Touchett speaks for everyone when she says, "There's nothing *of* him," and her son, Ralph, conveys what will happen when he tells Isabel, "You're going to be put in a cage." Why can she not see the obvious point for herself?

Isabel, the self-proclaimed seeker of an unrestricted view, has settled for a pompous fraud, one whose life is nothing but *"pose."* Osmond, as Isabel must later admit, has married her for her money. At his worst, in her ultimate realization of him, he wants "to surround his interior with a sort of invidious sanctity, to tantalise society with a sense of exclusion . . . not to please the world, but to please himself by exciting the world's curiosity and then declining to satisfy it." How could she have been so blind to these elements? James writes to make sure her defeat in marriage is total.

There are many reasons for Isabel's inability to see the truth, but they all come down to a defeat in perception that must be overcome. At a basic level, she knows Goodwood and can intuit the life of Warburton in orthodox terms. Osmond alone remains a mystery to be solved. She is therefore undone by her lack of knowledge, or, if you prefer, by her thirst for knowledge. In more thematic terms, the smart Isabel must suffer for a naive decision. She must be partially at fault. That is what defeat means.

Given Isabel's idealistic insistence on her total freedom to choose, knowledge through misery is likely, and it means a bad choice somewhere. "She became consistently wise," we learn early on, "only at the cost of an amount of folly." When Isabel resists Lord Warburton, by observing "I can't escape unhappiness" and wants to see for herself "what most people know and suffer," we realize she is in for it. Osmond provides negative experience, and James underlines the point by making him as odious as possible.

At a philosophical remove, Isabel's actions reflect the fleeting nature of possibility. Her hope for independent adventure leads her to reject Warburton and Goodwood. James chooses Isabel's hidden enemy, the former lover of Osmond, Madame Merle (the name means blackbird), to verbalize the quandary during their first meeting at Gardencourt: "You're young and fresh and of today; you've the great thing—you've actuality." Alas, actuality is a property soon lost. Serena Merle, the conniver who puts Isabel in Osmond's path, catches the essence: "I once had it—we all have it for an hour."

It may be that possibility is also an illusion. When Ralph says of Isabel, "she's as good as her best opportunities," he mistakenly thinks he can improve upon them by giving her a fortune against the better judgment of his dying father, the source of all largesse. A businessman, Mr. Touchett foresees "she may fall a victim of fortune-hunters." James already agrees through the language in Ralph's proposal. "I should like to put money in her purse," Ralph tells his father, a reminder of a more sinister manipulation. "Put money in thy purse" are Iago's words in betrayal of Shakespeare's Othello and Desdemona.

James painstakingly dramatizes the dilemma in possibility. Isabel, the archer, holds potential only as long as her bow is bent. When the arrow flies, it either hits its target or falls to earth; either way it is done. The newspaper woman in the novel, Henrietta Stackpole, is regularly ridiculed for her limited sensibilities, but she stands for practicality too, and she sees the dynamic involved. "Whatever life you lead," she tells Isabel, "you must put your soul in it—to make any sort of success of it; and from the moment you do that it ceases to be romance, I assure you; it becomes grim reality."

Maturity comes through heightened awareness of what one has seen. Isabel must learn to face the mistake that she has made directly and knowingly; otherwise, reality will become very grim indeed. She ponders her situation in the most remarkable realization scene in all of American literature.

Osmond has just left Isabel in the drawing room of their mansion, the Palazzo Roccanera in Rome. He demands that she lure her former admirer, Lord Warburton, into marriage with his daughter Pansy against Pansy's own wishes. This request exposes the narrow social climber for what he is, one who wants to be known as "the first gentleman in Europe," an empty title at the expense of others. Isabel naturally finds the assignment "a repulsive one." She has been asked to pimp for her husband's vulgar wishes.

Giving no answer to Osmond's request, Isabel remains still and alone in the room until four in the morning, "scanning the future with dry, fixed eyes." No longer hiding from the truth, she contemplates how "hideously unclean" Osmond has become, how he makes "everything wither that he touches," how he hates her, how dark her married life appears, how he has "almost malignantly . . . put out the lights one by one." This unsparing vision is horrifying, and it must be dealt with in some way, but how?

Isabel begins by readily accepting the role of her own ignorance as a first step in recovery from the defeat realized. In marrying Osmond, "she had not read him right," and recognition of the fault humbles her. Smart, she has not been smart enough, but she also sees that her mistake pales against "the magnitude of *his* deception."

Osmond's approach contained a veiled malice that a generous mind could not plumb. Beneath the surface, "his egotism lay hidden like a serpent in a bank of flowers."

The biblical reference has typological significance. Everyone, from the first couple in Eden, gets deceived; sham and subterfuge are part of life. Isabel wonders whether in joining the universal crowd she will suffer for "the rest of her life." Is she eternally condemned to "the house of darkness, the house of dumbness, the house of suffocation"? Nothing seems possible. "How could anything be a pleasure," she wails aloud, "to a woman who knew that she had thrown away her life?"

The important thoughts in Isabel's night vigil—"scanning the future with dry fixed eyes"—come in response to this overly melodramatic but devastating question about a life thrown away. The word "fixed" is key here. Isabel cannot afford to leave matters where they are. The set notion of "portrait" must not prevail. She must overcome "the incredulous terror with which she had taken the measure of her dwelling."

The deepest rewards in solitude flow from self-examination, but one must first know how to do it well. Isabel begins to recover by measuring her own character in relation to Osmond's, and the effort teaches her to think beyond her distress. Yes, she was defined in part by her love of ideas, but was not that "just what one married for, to share them with some one else"? She had married an ungenerous man out of generosity, but she had to admit, also out of the hypocritical desire to shift the burden of possibility in sudden wealth onto another. She made a disastrous miscalculation, but hadn't she done so out of her belief in possibilities? This language of self-scrutiny is the first aid.

Possibilities! Thought of Ralph Touchett, her intellectual soul mate, gives Isabel a glimpse of renewal. She remembers other arrows somewhere in the quiver that she, as the original archer and not as Mrs. Gilbert Osmond, has forgotten to send. Recalling Ralph's generosity of character opens Isabel to new thought beyond the present and outside of "the blasted circle round which she walked." Her intellectual efforts in the small hours of the night do not free her, but she no longer feels completely trapped. The saving knowledge of someone to share "made her feel the good of the world."

A new life begins to take hold when Isabel "disobeys" Osmond by returning to England to be with Ralph as he dies. Her eyes in the journey by train from Rome are "sightless" rather than "fixed." There is now an inner momentum in keeping with the motif of outward journey. Isabel has started to put the worst of the past behind her: "There was nothing to regret now—that was all over."

Reflection continues throughout the long journey to England. Isabel rediscovers herself by accepting the incremental value in life: "Deep in her soul—deeper than any appetite for renunciation—was the sense that life would be her business for a long time to come. . . . It was proof she should some day be happy again." She accepts that no one event should dominate an ongoing life. Defeat is one event. A truly active existence must engage with new opportunities as they offer themselves or impinge upon us.

The proof of Isabel's growth comes in the two death scenes at Gardencourt. Early in the novel, she shares the vigil over Mr. Touchett. The possibility that her newly discovered uncle might die in her presence is "an idea which excited her and kept her awake." The admission suggests more than distance from the dying man! Affection for Mr. Touchett, "a sort of golden grandfather" one step removed from "uncle," does not disguise that she is untouched by the suitably named Mr. Touchett.

Isabel is a young woman waiting for an old man to die in this scene in much the way that younger generations subliminally wait for nature to take its course. Ralph's foreshortened life and death from heart disease at novel's end presents another matter altogether. In this second, final vigil Isabel waits not for death, as she openly confesses, but in the hope, "full of tears and anguish," that the truth of her broken life might be accepted by the friend who has "been everything!"

Truth in this second death scene comes through an emotional bond, and it is achieved in the only real home that we receive in the novel. Having "lost all her shame, all wish to hide things" as she has done in the past, Isabel finds the right domestic space to forge ahead with new intellectual resolve. She must explain her misery to the one person who can share it: "Now he must know; she wished him to know, for it brought them supremely together, and he was beyond the reach of pain." Ralph already knows, but articulation between them is the recognition that both need.

One of the values of solitude lies in the ability to deliver what one has learned to another who shares a heightened grasp of experience. "You wanted to look at life for yourself—but you were not allowed," Ralph tells Isabel; "you were punished for your wish." "Oh, yes, I've been punished," she replies. She has been "ground in the very mill of the conventional," but recognition of this torment does not mean aspirations forever lost. Jamesian realism, always tougher than first imagined, insists on the value of continuing experience against the alternative of melodramatic pose.

Acceptance in this scene transcends the hurt in both individuals. Ralph's last words ratify what Isabel has already hoped for herself. "I don't believe that such a generous mistake as yours can hurt you for more than a little," he whispers. And he adds, "Remember this, that if you've been hated you've also been loved." The feeling exchanged has nothing to do with the romantic theme of love dominant in contemporary thought and literature. While few would deny the obsession with sexual adoration in today's world, the ultimate desire in adult life turns on more subtle concerns and moments.

James, in defining that adult life, sees what everyone really wants, and he gives it to Isabel in the last chapters of *The Portrait of a Lady*. The truest interest in human endeavor is to be understood, appreciated, and accepted by another. To be accepted in this way is to be kept valuably in mind. "Keep me in your heart," Ralph tells Isabel. "I shall be nearer to you than I've ever been."

Those around us who fail to apprehend and empathize at this level cannot be discarded, but neither should they be depended upon for the good life. "I never was what I should be!" Isabel cries anxiously in her most despairing moment of higher friendship with Ralph. His answering assurance is that she has been. She has been what she was capable of being, and it has been enough for him to understand and to love her for herself. Whether adrift or centered, surrounded or alone, happy or sad, in health or in illness, no one who has this much is ever completely alone.

Their Eyes Were Watching God

Janie Mae Crawford has none of Isabel Archer's opportunities, and yet the trajectory of her life is remarkably similar. Her personal growth also unfolds around three defective suitors: Logan Killicks, Joe "Jody" Starks, and Vergible "Tea Cake" Woods, and their defects present far greater risks than those Isabel faced from her suitors. Janie's social situation means that she must marry early for her own protection.

An impoverished, isolated, and attractive black girl in the South at the turn into the twentieth century,

Janie lives with vulnerabilities instead of possibilities. Her grandmother and mother before her have been brutally raped, and Janie knows she is the unwanted product of the second crime, which destroyed her mother's life. Still, and like Isabel, Janie achieves her full identity not through any of her marriages but through the recognition and goodwill of her closest friend.

Much has been made of Janie's development through storytelling, and rightly so, but Hurston's heroine knows how to tell a story long before anyone will bother to listen. "It takes two to speak the truth, one to speak and another to hear," writes Henry Thoreau in *A Week on the Concord and Merrimack Rivers.* Hurston's novel succeeds by giving Janie someone to hear the hidden value of her life. Her story must be told *and* heard by a sympathetic listener to be accepted as truth.

The seemingly passive listener in *Their Eyes Were Watching God,* Pheoby Watson, functions as much more than that. She is the mediating agent between Janie and a hostile community, and she answers to both. Pheoby's receptivity divides truth from the lies told about Janie. Both are aware of a "Mouth-Almighty" world bent on "mass cruelty." Named after Phoebe, the mythical goddess of the moon, Pheoby reflects Janie's light against the darkness of town gossip.

Janie, who is all alone but for this friendship, needs nothing beyond the honest affection and empathy in her audience of one, and she indicates her appreciation when she says, "Mah tongue is in mah friend's mouf."

From this beginning, Pheoby gives structure to Janie's story. "Eager to feel and do through Janie," she offers the receptivity and reciprocity that we all need. Pheoby unleashes "that oldest human longing—self revelation." The parallels in articulation are the same as in the first portrait of a lady. Janie talking and listening to Pheoby is as Isabel talking and listening to Ralph.

Janie Mae Crawford has every right to feel bitter against the world. She has lived more than half her life under the corrosive hatred of two husbands, and "in the meanest moment of eternity" she has been forced to kill her third husband, the only one who truly loved her. When Tea Cake contracts rabies from a mad dog and insanely attacks her with his pistol, she shoots him in self defense. Then, on "that same day of Janie's great sorrow," she must stand trial for murder with everyone "all against her."

Courage is when everyone is against you and you must act, when the many turn on the one: "So many were there against her that a light slap from each one of them would have beat her to death." We do not hear the story that Janie tells on the witness stand to save her own life. We know only that a unanimous black community wants her convicted and executed because her whiter looks have saved her: "dem white mens wuzn't gointuh do nothin' tuh no woman dat look lak her. . . . long as she don't shoot no white man."

Hurston brings a complicated mix of truth and falsehood to the black community's claim and, hence, to the problems in Janie's life. Although Janie has acted in such clear self-defense that any court in the land should exonerate her on the facts alone, she goes free on the basis of racist understandings. Found "not guilty" in five minutes by twelve white men, she is shielded from the swelling anger of the black community in singular fashion: "White women cried and stood around her like a protecting wall."

Speaking under hostile pressure in court refines the storyteller, and we sense it even though Hurston omits the story told. Instinctively but cleverly, Janie adjusts to the audience at hand, a more formal, public, intimidating, and larger audience than any she has ever known. "First thing she had to remember was she was not at home," Hurston notes, and in keeping with the public moment, the observation comes without any of the usual broken dialect from the character we know. Like any good speaker, Janie regulates her words to the listeners before her and with the inner resources of a life understood.

From birth Janie has been treated falsely in the world, and she has imbibed lessons from it. Her identity, slow in developing, has been refined by her resistance to the ignorance and malice all around her. Like Huckleberry Finn, she has learned to think for herself to get anywhere at all. Coping with tyranny in the home has made her a good counterpuncher. She knows the difficulty of getting unwilling people to see the truth. In Hurston's words, "She was in the courthouse fighting something and it wasn't death. It was worse than that. It was lying thoughts."

So adept is Janie Mae Crawford's presentation in a courtroom filled with people whose business is talk that no one responds or moves when she has finished speaking: "She had been through for some time before the judge and the lawyer and the rest seemed to know it." Hurston is giving us one more characteristic of the good storyteller with these words. Janie says only what is needed to demonstrate the integrity of her situation. All present are stunned by her cogency, her obvious sincerity, and her lack of artificial embellishment—all of which run counter to normal courtroom advocacy.

The novel confirms the power of what is said in court through the sharpened retelling Janie gives to Pheoby. We are listening to a twice-told tale, and the successful public speaker, now grounded in the comfortable privacy of her home, feels no pressure except the time needed to have her closest friend understand her. In asking for that time at the outset of the novel, Janie warns "'tain't no use in me telling you somethin' unless Ah give you de understandin' to go 'long wid it."

These words, the mark of the natural orator, settle Pheoby. "Dilated all over with eagerness," Pheoby supplies the virtues of a good listener: patience, attention, understanding, and sympathy. If Janie resists bitterness, it is through the enlarged view that the truth told and willingly received can furnish. Identity comes not only through the truth but in the knowledge of how to tell it well.

Janie's conclusions are the rounded life. "Ah done been tuh di horizon and back," Janie tells Pheoby, "and now Ah kin set heah in mah house and live by comparisons." She has had "de big convention of livin'," and no one can criticize her who has not done the same. "It's a known fact, Pheoby," Janie explains, "yuh got tuh *go* there tuh *know* there." The little girl of six who cannot recognize her own face in a photograph, who doesn't even realize that she is black and is ridiculed for it—"don't you know yo' ownself?"—speaks now as a woman who has taken the full measure of her world and herself in it.

The mutual advance of teller and listener lives in Pheoby's response. "Ah done growed ten feet higher from jus' listenin' tuh you, Janie," she says at the end. "Ah ain't satisfied wid mahself no mo'." No thoughtful person would want to endure what Janie has been through. Pheoby's words suggest instead the communicated value in Janie's life. She praises what Janie has become in the fire of experience.

Pheoby, the good listener, does more. She gives the teller another chance. Janie avoids despair through the true friendship that has offered her a new beginning. "Ah depend on you for a good thought," she tells Pheoby, who answers with the mutuality of meaning that true attention can provide. Pheoby confirms the light that her namesake, the moon, offers against fear of the night. At the last, in "finished silence," she has risen, "hugged Janie real hard and cut the darkness in flight."

Their Eyes Were Watching God, like *The Portrait of a Lady,* presents the difficulty in managing adulthood in moments of defeat. If youth in the American novel is about self-discovery, maturity is about doing one's best and hoping to be recognized for it by someone across the incremental patterns and attritions that force a life to move up and down through joy and sorrow.

Whatever the growth in Isabel Archer and Janie Mae Crawford, James and Hurston concentrate on hopes undone. Mr. Touchett, a source of wisdom as he is dying, reminds us that "things are always different from what they might be." Proving the point, Madame Merle lets her guard down just enough at Gardencourt to report on the inevitable damage in life. "You may depend on it that every one bears some mark," she observes. "I've been shockingly chipped and cracked," she confesses to Isabel, and she adds, "I do well for service yet, because I've been cleverly mended."

Actually Madame Merle has mended herself, and it is no mean accomplishment. We cannot admire her, but not for the last time she symbolizes the ways of the world. Hurston adds a more affecting version of the same phenomenon. Janie's grandmother at the bottom of the well of misery has been defeated at every turn in *Their Eyes Were Watching God.* As a former chattel shaped by slavery, she tells Janie "it wasn't for me to fulfill my dreams of whut a woman oughta be and to do." Be that as it may, these defeats do not define her. "Nothing can't stop you from wishin'," Nanny insists against the horrors in her life. "You can't beat nobody down so low til you can rob 'em of they will."

The fully engaged adult life must find the willpower to mend itself against the loneliness of personal defeat. Recovery may need the help of another, but it builds from recognitions in the self, a process made more difficult by the conventions of a civilization that gives defeat the back of its hand. The ultimate need for a reasoned solitude comes here. As James and Hurston prove, the American woman succeeds by thinking beyond her assigned situation and expected role. She cannot afford to leave herself to the portrait that others so willingly paint of her. The crafted surfaces may attract, but they hold defeat in place against the ability to look within and measure what is there.

5

EDITH WHARTON'S ANATOMY OF BREAKDOWN

Although personal breakdown takes different forms (injury, illness, mental disorder), the second syllable in the word supplies common ground. When we go down, we are less than we were, and others see us that way. We cannot do what we did before and struggle with aspects of life previously handled with ease. When that happens, and it eventually happens to all of us, a caretaker becomes necessary, and one of the problems becomes the nature of care taken under circumstances that nobody wants.

The Caretaker

The desire in breakdown is to get back, and depending on the gravity of the situation, the person undone must turn to others. But even when that person is surrounded by help, the situation pushes the sufferer onto the self in a new way. The limitations imposed drive the victim inward in search of relief. All ministrations then become double-sided: "care" in the name of the helper; "need" in the name of the helpless. Moreover, those who are healthy and those who are not think differently about the same things.

Curiously, then, American authors tend to treat the dialectic in breakdown as a simple add-on or plot convenience to move people around. Illness in Milly Theale motivates others in Henry James's novel *Wings of the Dove* (1902). We don't see illness or the treatment of it. We just know Milly has turned her face to the wall. Ernest Hemingway's "The Snows of Kilimanjaro" (1936) depends on a fatal infection from the scratch of a thorn. Physically helpless, Harry the protagonist falls into a feverish reverie as he dies. The injury is an enabling device, not the subject of the story.

F. Scott Fitzgerald may come closer than others in *Tender Is the Night* (1934). Mental disorder leads to reversals in strength between Dick Diver, doctor and husband to Nicole, the wife who leaves him for another man as she recovers. Nicole's mental illness remains a mystery glimpsed for other purposes in the novel. Admittedly, the glimpses are powerful. If Fitzgerald comes closer, it is because he sees the opportunity in the relationship of caretaker to patient when breakdown occurs.

The leading writer in American fiction on the theme is Edith Wharton in *The Fruit of the Tree* (1907). Her novel takes incapacity and treatment as its subjects, with drama arranged around an actual bed of pain. The topic therefore frightens more than it appeals, one reason why the raw power of the book is often overlooked. Wharton is generally taken as a novelist of manners who rewards people who are adept within their social milieu. This account has those elements, but it tells a very different kind of story. Wharton has written a classic novel of domesticity undone. She succeeds by casting her account in a caretaker who must make the decisions when, as not infrequently happens, a family collapses around her.

This protagonist, Justine Brent, is a nurse ambivalent about her calling. She appears torn between professionalism and personal levels of engagement, and the conflict is more acute in her because she is a single child who has recently lost her last parent and the home that went with it. The success of the novel depends on this hesitation in values and the relative isolation of one who is not undone by either problem.

In the central event, Justine's ambivalence leads her to euthanize a patient, Bessy Amherst, who is also her friend. When Bessy, paralyzed from a riding accident and kept artificially alive in irremediable pain, begs Justine to let her die, Justine covertly grants the request with an overdose of morphine, and Wharton seems to approve of the measure that has been taken. Justine does only what many a doctor surreptitiously arranges at the end of a life in unanswerable agony. Nonetheless, she must pay a high price for her act of mercy and is made to realize it at the expense of everything she cares about.

Wharton ends her novel on the theme with one of several allusions to the biblical significance of her title:

> Life is not a matter of abstract principles, but a succession of pitiful compromises with fate, of concessions to old tradition, old beliefs, old charities and frailties. That was what her act had taught her—that was the word of the gods to the mortal who had laid a hand on their bolts. And she had humbled herself to accept the lesson, seeing human relations at last as a tangled and deep-rooted growth, a dark forest through which the idealist cannot cut his straight path.

The passage confirms what we have always known. Justine is the only character in *The Fruit of the Tree* capable of thinking independently beyond social illusions. Her unique level of perception, the key to the novel, has led her to the forbidden knowledge of good and evil, and use of it has trapped her in the crisis of caretaking. Honest to a fault, Justine lies about her act of euthanasia. The lie, to be fair, covers a subject that American culture still refuses to face more than a century later, but in this case it requires Justine to end up living a related lie at the core of her marriage.

It is also true that flawed marriages proliferate everywhere in Wharton's fiction. They reflect the author's own unhappy union to the mentally imbalanced, unfaithful, mendacious, and financially corrupt Edward Robbins Wharton. In *The Fruit of the Tree*, though, Wharton clearly approves of the couple. Much more is at stake in this story of marriage against its background of spreading breakdown.

The Fruit of the Tree holds us in part because Justine Brent's ambivalence is Wharton's. Author and protagonist share a distaste for the sickroom, the pain in it, and those who cannot help themselves. Both ostracize the handicapped. The setting of the novel is 1907, before sophisticated analgesics against pain and long before communal norms try to help people with disabilities live a normal life.

For a horrifying account of what unarrested pain could mean at the time, one should read Henry Adams's extended description of his sister succumbing to lockjaw after bruising a foot in a carriage accident. "Hour by hour the muscles grew rigid while the mind remained bright, until after ten days of fiendish torture she died in convulsions." What changes Adams forever—"the terror of the blow stayed by him thenceforth for life"—is the meaningless infliction of such agony. "Nature enjoyed it, played with it, the horror added to her charm, she liked the torture, and smothered her victim with caresses." *The Education of Henry Adams,* privately circulated in the year Wharton published her novel, was probably available to her even earlier, and she would not have missed this "last lesson—the sum and term of education," in chapter nineteen with its title: "Chaos."

Wharton turns her own attention to how long-term care of another person isolates both sides of the relationship, the helper and the helpless. Many a spouse knows the lonely vigil over a failing mate in a life consumed by the attentions required, and an aging population faces more of such heartache. Prolongation of life has brought new meaning to caretakers and the length of time spent at bedside.

Justine Brent provides a good example of the caretaker. Already alone, she can do her lonely job without feeling the deprivation. At the same time, she is defined by her vulnerability in the solitude and supportive role that an intense patient relationship requires. She realizes "how easily she could be displaced" as the crisis approaches in chapter twenty-five, and finds herself "light and detachable as a dead leaf on the autumn breeze," hardly a positive self-image. The power in the novel comes in Justine's struggle to keep her balance. It is a struggle won, but again at a price that she must pay.

We can see just how much the caretaker drives Wharton's novel of domesticity on edge by the contrast in her leading ladies. Elizabeth Amherst, aptly known by the reductive "Bessy," is the beautiful blond lady in the mansion. She has married wealth and delights in the leisure of high society. Bessy also lacks intellect and stability. She is uncaring in her treatment of others, unable to be alone, and incapable of managing her own life. She needs others to control her ills and perpetual uncertainty. When crippled in a terrible accident, she is without resources against her pain and sudden isolation.

Justine Brent, the dark lady in the novel, is handsome, not beautiful; homeless; and of lower social standing in a service capacity. She is a nurse, or a lady's companion, or a governess until she wins Bessy's widower for herself. Always the same, she is defined by her intellectual interests, her ability to forge her own path, her ability to stand alone, and her desire to work for the benefit of others. As Wharton's heroine, she handles every social level while never losing sight of her own. The name "Justine" has no diminutive attached; in Latin it means righteous, just, or fair.

From the earliest pages of the novel, the ideal marriage would be between Justine and Wharton's male interest, John Amherst, of a comparable social background. Both come from formerly established families and so retain the social graces important to Wharton. Both possess a work ethic and reformist inclinations in contrast to the complacent rich whom they serve. Wharton places hurdles in the path of this ideal union but grants it in the end with the resources needed to pursue mutual goals.

There is, however, a twist in these arrangements. Justine is right to fear for her happiness. When her world crumbles in the blackmailing revelation of the doctor who knows her secret, her marriage to John Amherst joins the flawed ranks of others. Wharton predicts as much as early as chapter fourteen: "The tragic crises in wedded life usually turned on the stupidity of one of the two concerned; and of the two victims of such a catastrophe she felt most for the one whose limitations had probably brought it about."

Wharton offers a painful one-sided solution to this particular marital crisis. Justine proves strong enough to overcome the disastrous impact on her marriage by privately containing the lie in it. We are told at the end that "their personalities were more and more merged in their common work, so that, as it were, they met only by avoiding each other." But what kind of victory can this be, and how should we value it?

Critics debate where "the stupidity of one of the two concerned" resides in this marriage. Is Justine to blame for what she has done as caretaker in the sickroom and in agreeing to marry the man whose first wife she killed, or is John Amherst the stupid one for not realizing the necessity under which Justine felt compelled to act? The "limitations" all belong to Amherst, but either way, the deathbed, with Justine hovering over it, is the primal scene of the novel, and Wharton gives all her creative attention to it.

We see the nature of Wharton's preoccupation as she begins to write. Her tentative first title for the novel, *Atropos,* is a classical attribution. It refers to the Moirai, the three sister goddesses of antiquity who control the fate of mortals by assigning portions of good and evil.

Atropos is the third sister, the one who cuts the thread
of life.

The Bed of Pain

The focal point of the novel is foreshadowed in its first
pages. A factory worker named Dillon has had his hand
and arm mangled in a machine. Justine Brent, as nurse,
and John Amherst, assistant manager of the factory,
meet in the hospital over the victim's bed of pain. We
immediately learn that Justine's expertise differs from
that of the typical nurse but are not told whether this
difference means more or less.

Wharton carefully leaves the point hanging. Justine
"did not use, in speaking, the soothing inflection of her
trade." Nor does her "cool note of authority" hinder
"sympathy revealing itself only in the expert touch of
her hands and the constant vigilance of her dark steady
eyes," which "softened to pity as the patient turned his
head away with a groan." Just as quickly we learn that
Justine's "crowded yet lonely life" does not prevent
accurate "rapid mental classification of the persons
she met."

All these qualities lead Justine to agree with Amherst
that Dillon is now "useless lumber" and better off dead.
"I know what I should do if I could get anywhere near
Dillon," Amherst says, "—give him an overdose of morphine, and let the widow collect his life-insurance, and
make a fresh start." "I daresay," Justine responds, "poor

Dillon would do it himself if he could—when he realizes that all the good is gone." Both speak without any knowledge of the person they discuss.

Justine reveals two other elements in this first conversation that will figure in her later decision. "It's the curse of my trade," she tells Amherst, "that it's always tempting me to interfere in cases where I can do no possible good," and "I'm not fit to be a nurse—I shall live and die a wretched sentimentalist!" In fact, Justine is anything but sentimental. So what is a reader to make of so many crosscurrents? When the injured Dillon and his gravely ill wife are still around years later and thriving in chapter thirty-one, "admirably adapted to their new duties," how can we justify the earlier exchanges between Justine and Amherst about doing away with him?

Wharton holds our interest by making her heroine certain of what she has done and by placing her above all others. All qualms about her act of euthanasia come from other directions. To understand the power in this narrative strategy, we need to know how Justine's character works as the helpmate to others and why Wharton makes her the quickest as well as the deepest reader of those she does help.

In every instance Justine sees farther than anyone, and this is true even when people confuse her as Bessy often does. All of our sympathies go to the caretaker; none remain with the idle and childishly selfish patient done away with. So great is Wharton's craft in this disparity that Justine's "wave of anger" seems justified when Amherst assuages his own guilt by dedicating their common work to a false memory of his first wife.

The only person we consistently think well of in the novel is Justine Brent. A chapter-by-chapter approach reveals a golden paragon among people of clay. In chapter four, where others are confused, Justine "would have seen it all." In chapter seven, she is "the ringleader." In chapter nine, she lives above society but is transformed into the most attractive figure of it when given the right dress to match a voice that "seemed to shoot light." More than that, she triumphs as "the golden core of a pale rose," "so leaping with life" that she rises far above her "circle of well-to-do mediocrity."

Wharton's testimonials of delight never end. By chapter fourteen, Justine controls others through "precocious experience of life," and "clear view of life in the round," tinged as it is with "the light of imagination and penetrated by the sense of larger affinities." Philosophical range supports close expertise. "In Justine the personal emotions were enriched and deepened by a sense of participation in all that the world about her was doing, suffering, and enjoying; and this sense found expression in the instinct of ministry and solace."

How can we not trust this point of view in the absence of an alternative that we can respect? Wharton loads the dice in her favor long before it becomes time to gamble. Predictably, Justine is ready when the emergency occurs. In the moment of hearing about Bessy

Amherst's accident, she exhibits "miraculous lucidity of thought and action." The nurse in Justine sees with "the trained mind that could take command of her senses and bend them firmly to its service."

But what kind of service should be rendered? This is the question, and it awakens a contrasting trait beyond the nurse in Justine the friend, and the friend will use the nurse in the decision to be made. Typically, Justine is already master of the contrast in her makeup, and it contains a warning for her that she will have to consider in the crisis. In the same moment as Bessy is brought in, she acknowledges too much sympathy for her patients and calls it "the joint in her armour."

Authorial intensity and preoccupation with the ensuing death scene take an interesting structural form. Justine's decision to relieve the fatally suffering Bessy occupies the center of the novel: chapters twenty-six through twenty-nine out of fifty-three chapters overall, but with a telling discrepancy. Wharton seems to lose creative energy after the pivotal event. Chapters after the crisis are shorter, hurried chronologically, and far more abrupt in tone. The structural second half of the novel fills less than a third of its pages.

By design, the crucial middle chapters work hard to exonerate the decision-maker. The fatal fall from the horse occurs because Bessy Amherst, irrationally angry with her husband and friend, ignores their advice in a self-destructive manner. The fall is the result of foolish behavior and the victim's own fault. Wharton also removes all direct familial decision-makers from the scene of suffering, and everyone professionally involved knows the injuries are fatal ones. The only question left to discuss over the bed of unbearable pain is "when will the patient die?"

Justine is left at bedside with a limited younger physician who feeds off of the praise of established colleagues for prolonging a life that cannot be saved. Dr. Wyatt is suspect in other ways. He is a dope addict, and a flawed suitor of Justine. Now she sees more. "To the young physician Bessy was no longer a suffering, agonizing creature: she was a case—a beautiful case." As Bessy's pain grows uncontrollable, Justine comes to detest Wyatt. He proceeds like "a skilled agent of the Inquisition" in calculating "how much longer the power of suffering might be artificially preserved in a body broken on the wheel."

More tangible factors support Justine's decision to end hopeless suffering. Bessy uses her lucid moments to ask for death. The passing days have turned her into "a mere instrument on which pain played its incessant deadly variations," and she continues to plead for death until her "wailing" and "moaning" are "no longer the utterance of human pain, but the monotonous whimper of an animal."

It is the friend not the nurse who decides to act, but with the nurse's medical knowledge and with the tacit support of the still absent husband, John Amherst, who has once encouraged just such an act in the clearest possible language and asked her, "Don't you ever feel tempted to set a poor devil free?"

Timeless philosophy lends further support to the exigency of the moment. Amherst, a regular reader of Shakespeare and other major thinkers, has left notes behind that "seem to represent his beliefs." Some of his jotted notes are from Pascal's *Pensées*: "La vraie morale se moque de la morale"—loosely, "true morality mocks conventional morality." In her emotional extremity but with a free-ranging mind that sees farther than "accepted forms, inherited opinion," Justine performs the act of mercy that will not quite ruin her life. Not quite. That tempered distinction is crucial to Edith Wharton's purposes.

Recovery

Exposure, rather than personal guilt—a clear departure from the blame heaped on the first couple in Eden—drives the remaining pages in *The Fruit of the Tree*. Wharton uses the distinction to pit innovative thought against the questionable norms of society, and the keeper of the imbalance in this equation, the exposer, is made as despicable as possible in the drug-addicted, wheedling figure of Dr. Wyatt. Justine's own view never wavers. "From the first," she decides when blackmailed by Wyatt, "she had retained sufficient detachment to view her act impartially, to find it completely justified by circumstances."

Justine's miscalculation is in another direction. She has mistaken the man who has now become her husband. She has put too much confidence in John Amherst's "independence of traditional judgments," and by chapter thirty-six she must face "the stony image that sat in her husband's place." When questioned by him, she answers "proudly, strongly." "I didn't care for the others—and I believe that, whatever your own feelings were, you would know I had done what I thought was right."

Unfortunately, Amherst cannot rise to this level of comprehension. Blackmail, rather than any sense of doubt, makes Justine realize "what I had done might be turned against me," and this perception makes her "afraid for my happiness." Amherst's timidity over proprieties destroys that happiness for both.

Wharton's major philosophical claim in the second half of *The Fruit of the Tree* projects this loss of happiness. After marital separation of a year, Justine next appears before her husband as the nurse serving others that she had no longer wanted to be, and the cost to her is made obvious. Her "healthy reed-like strength now suggested fatigue and languor. And her face was spent, extinguished—the very eyes were lifeless."

Wharton plays in this scene upon the classical meanings of her heroine's name. Justine, still fair and just, reminds Amherst "of some antique bust," and the frozen image is relevant in plot terms too. Justine has realized that her husband is not the soul mate she thought she had married. She now stands alone, a reserved statue even when with him.

Wharton is particularly interested in what standing alone means at the end. Justine continues the life of service that has always been her impulse in common effort with the husband she rejoins. Missing is the joy that real companionship can bring, and Justine, as we last see her, stoically accepts that condition. She sees there can be no mutual understanding of the level of thought that she has achieved. We again have a house without a home; professional commitment without the comfort of domesticity.

We leave Justine "pledged to the perpetual expiation of an act for which, in the abstract, she still refused to hold herself to blame." Life, of course, is not lived in the abstract. Even so, Justine's continuing acts of service are part of her ongoing nature rather than a form of penance. In the most important variation from the biblical account in Genesis, she has eaten of the fruit of the tree of knowledge but lives blameless in her own mind against conventional understandings of the story.

Wherein, then, does expiation lie? It lies in Justine's silence, in her willingness to bend outwardly to the norms of her society, in her official public and domestic regard for the man who has betrayed the adventure in thought that she thought they had shared. Disappointment rather than disaster is the result.

Is there wisdom in this deliberately tepid conclusion? We all break down sooner or later and need help when it happens. In a passage of *Pensées* not given by Wharton but surely known to her, Pascal observes "the natural misfortune of our mortal condition is so great that when we consider it closely nothing can console us." Justine Brent considers that condition closely and comes away whole from it. There is everything to admire in her tenacious strength and even more in her decision to live within her own counsel about it. Wharton means for us to see and arrange the possibilities when things turn against us.

In *Ethan Frome,* four years later in 1911, Wharton returns obliquely to the issues of breakdown. This time, she leaves everyone in a far more appalling situation: an endless long-term care arrangement across decades of ruin and frustration. Mattie, the kind young cousin brought in to help Ethan's wife Zeena, a professional invalid, has become a monster of need and anger herself after a willful event leaves her paralyzed and Ethan badly hurt. The injuries mirror Bessy Amherst's accident, but this time the patients live on and on in a town suitably named Starkfield. Zeena must now become the caretaker for people who had been assigned the task of taking care of her. The ugly reciprocities in Wharton's story suggest that everyone must take a turn.

There is much to worry about in breakdown. When it happens, as it will, independent strength of mind is a vital resource in caretaker and patient alike. One of Justine Brent's problems in the crucial decision she makes lies in her confirmed realization that Bessy Amherst lacks that strength. Justine has been acting for both of them and continues to do so over the bed of pain. Wharton suggests that whether such an action is right or wrong depends on circumstance rather than conventions that are of little help in the difficult moments individuals must face in actual experience.

We are left with Justine's self-possession and a remaining question, first raised in chapter nine of *The Fruit of the Tree* over the sources of Justine's "sound nature." We learn there that she has promised "to do her part in the vast impersonal labour of easing the world's misery." That accepted task is too large for anyone; the lesson is in the effort made. John Amherst's failure and Justine's miscalculation about him come in what he cannot see even when placed in a vocational context of greater vision and possibility.

Justine relies on John Amherst's apparent idealism when she acts over Bessy's bed of pain. She assumes "close contact with many forms of wretchedness had freed him from the bondage of accepted opinion," but the opposite remains true of him. Amherst's failure is the result when someone faces a new challenge with old thought, and the failure is one more illustration of the unusual quality in Justine's point of view. No reader has to agree with what she has done to note her continuing strength when her action is revealed to a world that refuses to understand it.

Wharton's heroine survives as a self-contained intellect who nonetheless continues to give of herself to others without the need of recognition or reward and without losing her balance when criticized. Still a caretaker, she has learned not to lean on the opinion of other people in the definition of her actions, even as she continues to help them. These are not small strengths. They are the elements of solitude that protect us against the burdens of care. If we are to believe Edith Wharton, an exceptional maturity of thought and the balances it provides are the gifts offered against breakdown but rarely taken.

MIDPOINT: THE LORDS OF LIFE REVISITED

The lords of life—*failure, betrayal, change, defeat, breakdown, fear, difference, age,* and *loss*—appear at any point and often in combination against us, but they gradually become more distinct in the life cycle, and the four that remain for analysis are less episodic in extent than enduring. *Fear, difference, age,* and *loss* bring more insistent challenges the longer we live. It is, after all, the matured Emerson, at forty-one, who coins the phrase and explains the concept. "I am not the novice I was fourteen, nor yet seven years ago," he tells us just after listing "the lords of life" as "threads on the loom of time." He also says this: "The years teach much which the days never know."

In this essay, "Experience," we have what critics agree is Emerson's most sophisticated stand against the troubles in existence. There have been earlier tragedies in life for Emerson—the death of his first wife, Ellen Tucker Emerson, and of his closest brother, Charles—but the loss of his beloved son Waldo in 1842 gives the impetus to "Experience" two years later in 1844. The death of Waldo drives Emerson into a unique expression of personal grief, and the essay itself becomes our benchmark because, more than any other writing that can be named, it presents the philosopher of "self-reliance" battling to sustain his creed against human limitations that he must now acknowledge in painful detail.

"Experience"—literally the attrition the years bring—pulls no punches in the restrictions that the writer now sees. "Gladly would we anchor, but the anchorage is quicksand," Emerson admits, while also disclosing that "the whole frame of things preaches indifferency." "Life itself is a bubble and a skepticism, and a sleep within a sleep. . . . a flitting state, a tent for a night." Even the gift of perception proves faulty. "As I am, so I see; use what language we will, we can never say anything but what we are." Trapped in this prism of self, "the life of truth is cold and so far mournful." Emerson has discovered we are alone in a world that has no plan to care for us. "God's darling!" he sneers at his reader, "heed thy private dreams; thou wilt not be missed in the scorning and skepticism." There is a new problem in being alone.

"The soul is not twin-born but the only begotten." It admits "no co-life."

Emerson, in accepting this starker level of isolation, will rely only on *"that which is its own evidence."* He is in tacit retreat from the more expansive apostle of self-reliance. "I have set my heart on honesty in this chapter," he promises, and this means he will only measure out the value actually left to us. Because we are often deluded in what we see, we cannot afford to "look other than directly and forthright." Thereby, "we do what we must and call it by the best names we can." Reductive tones and terms are everywhere. Whether life is "sick or well," our job is "to finish that stint." If we are limited to moments, "let us husband them."

Although the positives in "Experience" are harder won, Emerson's customary nonlinear prose style allows him to intersperse "limitations of the affirmative statement" at will. So while the path we "must walk is a hair's breadth," the surprises in life are still what make it worth living. Significant possibilities remain: "We have not arrived at a wall, but interminable oceans." "The spirit is not helpless or needful of mediate organs." "In liberated moments we know that a new picture of life and duty is already possible."

How is it possible? The word "self-reliance" has been replaced by a new phrase, "the capital virtue of self-trust." Admittedly, the new terminology provides less scope—"we must hold hard to this poverty, however scandalous"—but the power of imagination still saves us even though the turn inward is now different: "Leave me alone and I should relish every hour and what it brought me, the potluck of the day." This more subdued celebrator of solitude is more cautious. He says instead, "I am thankful for small mercies." "Patience and patience," he cries, "we shall win at the last."

If Emerson is shaken, the more tentative answers offered continue to rely on the solitude available to anyone who will learn to trust its real power. Much of what we do and think is easily forgotten, "but in the solitude to which every man is always returning, he has a sanity and revelations which in his passage into new worlds he will carry with him." We retain the knowledge of ourselves and the unique thoughts that go with that realization. True vigor in thought can "fill up the vacancy between heaven and earth." But what if the vacancy between heaven and earth remains, as it seems to now? Emerson, in a telling conflation of positive and negative imagery, stands us on our own feet and in our own territory. Whatever our limitations, we are "the God the native of these bleak rocks."

These and other words bring us to the edge of modernity, where different kinds of answers will be given to the same problems. They also suggest something important about the lords of life. No matter what we believe, we are alone with them. Nature is no longer mediate or cooperative, as the younger Emerson felt. As he now agrees in "Experience," "Nature does not like to be observed, and likes that we should be her fools and playmates." Lest the point be missed, he inserts, "Nature, as we know her, is no saint." Hard words for the writer of *Nature* back in 1836, but it would make no difference now if Nature remained benevolent. The ultimate lords of life are not triggered by the world. They exist within us. We cannot help their presence. They are always there, and we cannot evade them or put them aside. The remaining struggles haunt us in a different way and require a more lasting brand of courage.

Emerson cleverly shuffles the lords of life at the end of "Experience" in order to demonstrate their bewildering power over us. Accordingly, in our own renaming of those to be taken up next, we must accept the tenuous grasp we have on them. *Fear* is an unavoidable instinct tied to self-preservation. Anyone can be undone by it suddenly and in numerous ways. *Difference* challenges our understanding at every step of the way. It is equal parts luminous perception and invidious distinction as we cope with a world that shifts on us in the thrust of time. If *Age* comes to those who live long enough, it withers without remedy. *Loss* is the worst of all. It replenishes every challenge we have already met.

Only the measured life can confront these elements, and the means are mysterious. All we can do is struggle for a better understanding of ourselves and what we have been to others. Emerson is surely right that we are alone with whatever healing powers of solitude we have managed to create and sustain in ourselves. At our best, we search for a way to make ourselves whole and accountable even as we stumble.

Literature is more than an example in this search. It is the path of shared understanding and the one affirmation that cannot be taken away as long as we are aware of it. When all else fails, it is the home for the mind. Story and song complete us in glimpses and moments. In their arrangement and capacity to move us, they carry beyond the noise of the day into the realms of perception, mindfulness, form, rhythm, and sensibility. They demonstrate meaning in the claim of completion. The good account supplies the rounded life, and we see afresh when that happens. In "To Homer," Keats captures the essence of Emerson's "new worlds." "Aye," the poet cries, "on the shores of darkness there is light":

> There is a budding morrow in midnight;
> There is a triple sight in blindness keen.

6

THE IMMIGRANT NOVEL: FEAR IN AMERICA

If you have never been seriously afraid, you have not lived. We all know what fear is, and it is easy enough to find in fiction. Even children's stories depend on at least a tincture of dread. But if one can find it in any story, it is best studied in a visceral form, and this characteristic proliferates and ultimately defines the immigrant novel. There is no apprehension quite like the journey from home lost to home unknown, and we will encounter it again in the Middle Passage of African American slavery in Chapter 7.

Overwhelming disquiet, disjuncture, and loneliness accompany an immigrant's entrance into America. Fear is the logical impulse when everything is unknown. Dislocation, nostalgia for what has been left, vocational struggle, language difficulty, new ideological assumptions, discrimination, poverty, sacrifice, and bewildering expectations—they are the elements that dominate the immigrant narrative, dividing families, friends, neighbors, and workers in anxiety and turmoil.

These emotions frequently undercut the dreams that brought a person here. No matter how hard a family of immigrants tries, some of its members go under, drop behind, or choose a transgressive path in trying to cope. The new home is never the old home. Disparities develop, mistreatment is a given, and the effort to adjust threatens the identity of all. No other form in the American novel insists quite so stridently on the unfairness in history. Loss and regret are defining characteristics, the calling cards of the genre.

Canonical works all prove these points. O. E. Rölvaag's *Giants in the Earth* (1927), a story of Norwegian settlers in the Dakota Territory of the 1870s, ends with strangers finding the grotesquely thawing corpse of Rölvaag's protagonist sitting on a haystack months after family quarrels have sent him into a snowstorm on a hopeless errand of mercy. The sequels in this trilogy, *Peder Victorious* (1929) and *Their Fathers' God* (1931), track the disintegration of immigrant families beset by economic uncertainty, ethnic prejudice, natural disasters, and religious intolerance.

Escape from these problems and fears is never without a return in the immigrant novel. Set in New York's

Lower East Side, Anzia Yezierska's *Bread Givers* (1925) recounts Sara Smolinsky's struggles with a tyrannical father, a rabbi who selfishly ruins the lives of his two older daughters. Sara alone escapes, but her success means she must take this abusive father into her own house. "If he lives with us," she warns her husband in desperation, "we will lose our home." The last words of the novel say a good deal more: "I felt the shadow still there, over me," Sara protests. "It wasn't just my father, but the generations who made my father whose weight was still upon me."

Even success extracts measures of trepidation and depression. Abraham Cahan's *The Rise of David Levinsky* (1917) depends on the irony in its title. Emotionally stunted and alone from his climb as a poor Talmudic student in Europe into a wealthy cloak-manufacturer in America, Levinsky treasures only his lost boyhood. "I can never forget the days of my misery," he concludes. Nothing pleases him. "I pity myself for a victim of circumstance," he explains in the end. "There are moments when I regret my whole career, when my very success seems to be a mistake."

Each of these writers focuses on a part of the problem, but the concluding tones are the same: discomfort, alienation, and a consuming monody of sorrow. The title of Mario Puzo's immigrant novel, *The Fortunate Pilgrim* (1964), is similarly ironic in implication. Puzo's heroine, a pillar of strength, declaims from reservoirs of sorrow.

"America, America, what different bones and flesh and blood grow in your name?" cries Lucia Santa, as she buries a husband who now means nothing to her. "My children do not understand me when I speak, and I do not understand them when they weep."

Every immigrant novel is tortured by the imperative of assimilation, the assumption that the melting pot of America will solve the problems of difference, but nothing is more impossible within the generational moment. At her mother's funeral in *Bread Givers,* Sara finds "a hundred eyes burned on me in their condemnation" when she fails to rend her garment in the traditional expression of grief. It means nothing to the elderly enforcers around her that she wears her only suit for work. "Look at her, the *Americanerin!*" sneer the ghetto mourners. "A lot she cares for her mother's death."

The immigrant novel naturally looks back. It is retrospective in its play on the shift that has taken place between cultures. Realized travail is its charge. There is, however, a vibrant exception. Henry Roth's underground classic *Call It Sleep* from 1934 tells a similar story but from the flashing immediacy of a small child. We cannot avoid the utter proximity of fear and loneliness in a character who is bewildered at every moment. It catches and sustains our attention in a unique way.

David Schearl, whom we see only between the ages of two and eight, lives in continuous terror of both the known and unknown worlds around him, and he learns to hide his own knowledge from those around him.

"Everything he knew frightened him," we learn early in the novel. Fear forces this "quiet, quiet child" inward onto his own inevitably mistaken terms. Even his image in a mirror can scare him. No other character in American fiction spends quite so much time thinking without speaking. David's mother, Genya, finds her son so unresponsive that she says, "I really believe you think of nothing." The opposite, of course, is true. Fear turns his mind into a silent but racing engine of concern.

Genya, like everyone else in the novel, even though she knows him best, misses the depth in David when she asks, "You see, you hear, you remember, but when will you know?" The questions in the novel are *how* will David know, and from *whom* will he take it? Consuming uncertainty is the measure of his fear.

Roth's modernist novel is laced with structural innovations. Sudden breaks in narrative give the trajectory of the text jagged edges in keeping with David Schearl's moments of panic under stress. Linguistic byplay, quick bursts in other languages, street slang, abrupt symbolism, and sudden misconnections capture the prejudice and violence of ghetto life and David's vulnerability in it. We are as confused as David at times, and our unsettled state blends with his bewilderment.

Two cohering elements give *Call It Sleep* a spontaneity often lacking in the genre of the immigrant novel. First, Roth insists on a stark presentism using stream of consciousness techniques, and second, his child protagonist holds us within a limited but always perceptive point of view. As the first element encourages confusion and awareness to chase each other across the page, so the second element turns the vulnerability of childhood into the puzzle of the immigrant experience.

The puzzle also serves an epistemological purpose. The child's consuming anxiety and fears are those of anyone forced to deal with unknowns that are too important to ignore. Fear, in this sense, belongs to the limits of knowing in a universe that appears too immense to care or be known. In parallel terms, the universe that David Schearl quite reasonably fears in its size and unresponsiveness is America itself.

The boy's very name bespeaks the fear that coming to America creates in his life. "David" means "beloved," a symbol of his mother Genya's obsessive devotion, while the patronymic "Schearl" is Yiddish for "scissors," and it stands for the cutting anger of his father Albert. Albert Schearl's violent rages have two sources in *Call It Sleep*. He has been unable to adapt to life in America, and two years of separation from his wife allow him to suspect the young son who he fears may not be his own.

In trying to fathom an adult world that is only half understood even by the adults around them, children are at once the most adaptable, the most vulnerable, and the most frantic of immigrants. Questions are the dominant mode of a child, and David Schearl is filled with them; but unlike other children, he dares not ask them in his divided household. Instead the questions tumble inward, only half articulated in thought.

Roth uses the withheld in this frightened child to expose conflict in the immigrant experience for what it is, a familial landscape of ferocious intensity. All of David's fears are confirmed in the end. The indelible image that he holds of his father is of a raised hammer poised to strike, and it will turn into the truth of the book. In a final cataclysm, Albert loads every misfortune onto the belief that David is "a goy's get" rather than his own son. "Whirling the whip in his flying hands," he tries to kill the son who is so different from himself and becoming more different every day.

Critics have tried to verify Albert's assumption about the paternity of David, but in the momentums of immigration, Albert has no son and certainly not the son he thinks he needs. America, not biology, has taken the son from the father. In introduction to others, Albert objectifies David as "what will pray for me after my death," a reference to the Jewish tradition of a son who remembers and prays after his father, but Albert is raising a son who sees only "the face of a foe." The only thing David wants from his father is the same physical strength in order to be free of him.

Chilling indifference and vortices of fear define the world beyond the home. The boy's first expressed thoughts are devastating in their portrayal of the immigrant condition: "David again became aware that this world had been created without thought of him." Every immigrant experiences this alienation from a new reality. The receiving world has no reason to make room, and its rhythms do not care for the latest perceiver of them.

All of the struggle to understand, all of the adjustments in order to belong, all of the effort to be understood must be made by the new arrival, and David can do so only with a warped and internalized miscomprehension. Quick to perceive, he lacks a context for understanding. There may be no greater terror for a keen observer than the need to know against the knowledge that you cannot learn what is important to know.

The misunderstandings, mistakes, abuse, guilt, and prejudices that guide the immigrant plot toward catastrophe are all heightened by the stream of consciousness that Roth uses to convey the psychological thought processes of a figure defined by "watchful, frightened eyes." Silent except when forced to speak in the confusion of languages available to him, David can find no purchase in a world against him. Lost in the city, he jumbles his thought processes when taken to a police station:

> Trust nothing. Trust nothing. Trust nothing. Wherever you look, never believe. If you played hide'n'-go-seek, it wasn't hide'n'-go-seek, it was something else, something sinister. If you played follow the leader, the world turned upside down and an evil force passed through it. Don't play.... Never believe. Never play. Never

> believe. Not anything. Everything shifted. Everything changed. Even words. . . . Trust nothing. Even sidewalks, even streets, houses, you looked at them. You knew where you were and they turned. You watched them and they turned. That way. Slow, cunning. Trust no'—.

David lives by a controlling insight. He must hold himself apart to survive, and there is pathos in how lonely he has become in that recognition. The compounded negatives in his thoughts convey impossible levels of disbelief, isolation, and doubt. David's alienation carries to every level of implication; people, words, buildings, even play are all suspect. Transferring the anger in his home to the world, the lost boy is convinced that the expanding dimensions around him are openly accusatory. The whole world has animate force, and it is ranged against him with malevolent intent.

The rapid linear sequence of juxtaposed phrases in the passage builds David's terror into a palpable force, but it also conveys a secret "cunning." The power of Roth's novel lies in our awareness of an alienated and necessarily fragmented mind constantly at work but misfiring because so determinedly alone and afraid. The strength of intellect in an innocent child is our guide. Whatever has gone wrong, no reader can place the wrong in David Schearl. We cannot expect the boy to do better than he does.

Looking to this strength of mind, some readers have found a semiotic bildungsroman of growth in David's mastery of the language mix in *Call It Sleep* (his precocious knowledge of Yiddish, English, and especially Hebrew, but *not* the Polish of his parents' land). Others use Roth's interwoven Jewish and Christian references to create a unified symbol system. Still others rely on the ghetto setting to see a working-class novel with David as the avatar of labor movements. Psychoanalytic approaches emphasize Oedipal implications. Cultural critics give David the childhood of a New World messiah.

Mythic subtexts and insertions of the spiritual in ordinary life—modernist techniques that Roth borrows from T. S. Eliot and James Joyce—have encouraged the widest interpretive range. More than anything, though, the novel turns on the survival of a small boy teetering on the brink in a world he dreads more than he inhabits.

From the outset, *Call It Sleep* privileges negative shocks of recognition in the immigrant's plight. The book opens with the symbolic placement of Genya and David "in wonder" before the Statue of Liberty, but their wonder is negative rather than the conventionally assumed scene of awe on arrival. Neither mother nor child sees a welcoming beacon of light. In splintered fragments of prose "the massive figure" of the statue looms above them "charred with shadow"; her halo "sparks of darkness roweling the air"; her torch "the blackened hilt of a broken sword." Genya's articulation is correspondingly bleak. "Ach!" she cries. "Then here in the new land is the same old poverty."

Roth's child protagonist lives in permanent alarm as he endures trauma after trauma in a confusing and openly threatening ghetto of mutually antagonist immigrant groupings, and he is eventually driven beyond all endurance. As David is walking home toward what he expects to be certain doom—a reality avoided only by extraordinary interventions—his mind approaches total collapse. So beaten down is the boy that he merges his identity in the objects of the store windows that he passes. Roth's broken phraseology is horrifying in its capacity to illustrate a fragmenting mind flying out of control:

> Only his own face met him, a pale oval, and dark, fear-struck, staring eyes, that slid low among the windows of the stores, snapping from glass to glass, mingled with the enemas, ointment-jars, green globes of the drug-store— snapped off—mingled with the baby clothes, button-heaps, underwear of the drygoods store—snapped off—with the cans of paint, steel tools, frying pans, clothes-lines of the hardware store—snapped off. A variegated pallor, but pallor always, a motley fear, but fear. Or he was not.
>
> —On the windows how I go. Can see and ain't. Can see and ain't. And when I ain't, where? In between them if I stopped, where?

> Ain't nobody. No place. Stand here then. BE
> nobody. Always. Nobody'd see. Nobody'd know.
> Always. Always No.

The passage makes windows "happen" to the boy instead of receiving his movement across them. They
"snap off," and the shift in agency allows David to dissolve when his reflection does not appear in them. Pas-
sivity of this kind can trouble any stranger momentarily
on unfamiliar terrain, but David is permanently estranged and much more deeply hurt. He no longer exists or wants to exist. "Ain't nobody. No place." Even
worse, he asks directly to "BE nobody."

The traumatized boy cannot find his own place in
things. Caught between home and the street without the
means of bringing them together, David suffers from
disassociations familiar to a new foreign-born resident,
but they are magnified in him by the calamity of total
rejection at every level, even though nothing that happens is his fault. The brilliance in Roth's use of the child
protagonist lies here in the creation of an innocent figure
who can think everything *is* his fault. Trudging toward
the home that is always a domestic battleground, David
Schearl is *immigrant agonistes*. He is the quintessential
alien, alienated even from himself, and we can only ask
rather hopelessly, who or what will help?

Roth's answer comes in an astounding affirmation
out of relentless negation. Throughout *Call It Sleep* the

separate denizens of the street have been animated by anti-Semitism, malice, theft, confrontation, ridicule, and cruelty, but they miraculously join together and come to the rescue at novel's end. Roth posits a subliminal goodwill in the common denominator of the people, not an unusual assumption in either American fiction or American politics. This collectivized sense of virtue is not explained, but it lives in the sporadic exchanges of the misfits and hangers-on that help David.

David nearly dies twice; first, under the uncontrolled blows of his father—"Let me strangle him! Let me rid the world of a sin!"—and then in panic-stricken flight into the uncaring streets of New York. Running away from "a reeling smear of words, twitching gestures, fractured lights, features, a flickering gauntlet of tumult and dismay," the terrified boy reaches for the guiding hand he has never had. He unleashes the only alternative source of power he has ever seen, and there is authorial purpose in making that source mechanical in origin rather than human. The machinery of industrial America is the immigrant's resort, the clearest tool for initial advancement, and all too often, a zone of peril and misfortune.

Peril is the result here. David's father has become a milkman, and the boy inserts the father's steel milk dipper into the live third rail of railroad tracks near his home, nearly electrocuting himself in his desperate quest for alternative meaning. Knocked unconscious and badly burned, David is saved by the unlikeliest of sources.

Street people, the inhabitants of Roth's personal version of T. S. Eliot's Waste Land, join hands to recover the boy and restore him to his home, led by a medical intern and a stock Irish policeman.

This last scene gives us Roth's ambiguous, much-discussed title. Spurned, nearly electrocuted, burned and filled with "torpid heart-break" on his bed of pain, the boy hears his mother say, "You'll go to sleep and forget it all." We know that he will forget nothing, and he tells us so when he thinks without saying, "One might as well call it sleep," with the added phrase "it was only toward sleep that he knew himself." A mantra repeated over and over again by the boy who watches everything around him through carefully half-closed eyes, these phrases complete the book. As always, David's thoughts are not shared with anyone, and they contradict what has been said to him.

What do these mysteriously reiterated phrases finally mean? David, in his isolation and vulnerability, is defined by three levels of mental engagement: he learns to welcome being alone in his loneliness as the safest place to be; he thinks for himself in a way that both answers and compounds confusion; and he is deeply distressed by what he does not know. As he realizes, "His mind would fly apart if he brought no order into this confusion. . . . Not knowing became almost unbearable." The novel depicts that "flying apart," and there may be no livelier type for anyone left in ignorance against his will. How can you know if no one cares enough to tell you what should be known?

"Call it sleep," as opposed to sleep, suggests what the thinker of the phrase is beginning to become. The words define an active mind still carefully hidden from others but at last a little less hidden from itself. The endangered boy begins to find himself in the privacy that the pretense of sleep creates in a crowded room. He has learned it is unsafe to speak, and so once again he remains proverbially silent, but this time the silence is more calculated than before, and the closed prism of apprehension in which he lives is "not terror, but strangest triumph, strangest acquiescence."

What is here to build upon? Roth offers a tentative answer. He points repeatedly to an underlying strength of mind despite the confusion of its owner. When David gives an inspired reading in Hebrew, his rabbi drums the boy's forehead with a blunt finger and finds "an iron wit." Will that be enough? Perhaps not, but there is more. David, even at the age of eight, has learned how to be alone. He has learned how to think for himself, and, a true seeker, he is troubled by not knowing.

These are not small achievements. We cannot be sure in such a troubled child, but there is an element of hope in what David Schearl says to himself as the domestic scene of home is reestablished in the final moments of the novel: "It was only toward sleep one knew himself." The future hinges on the knowledge of self

that contemplation can provide. The mind that hereto-
fore can "trust nothing" has begun to conquer its unre-
strained fears by trusting itself. Always alone, the boy
has suddenly learned *how* to be alone. He has discovered the value in a working solitude, and against every
problem that remains, it is the beginning of a life worth
living.

7

WILLIAM FAULKNER AND TONI MORRISON
PLOT RACIAL DIFFERENCE

Prejudice based on human difference appears in the Constitution of the United States for all to see, and no one under the continuing protection of that document escapes involvement in the history behind it. Centuries of legally justified racial injustice have caused most Americans to acknowledge the fact of discrimination but not its continuing power or the more fundamental impulse behind it.

That impulse is the polar opposite in conception to what the psychotherapist Alfred Adler termed "the inferiority complex," and it applies to everyone rather than individual personality disorders. A more hidden but pervasive "superiority complex" is the source of individuation in forming personal identity, but it is also the force behind discrimination, conflict, disorder, and injustice in communal life, and it may have special appeal within the leveling tendencies of a democratic society.

The superiority complex celebrates difference. Everyone, it seems, needs someone to look down upon, whether because of race, status, ability, class, ancestry, association, ownership, vocation, intelligence, fortune, family, education, gender, or simple dumb luck. No one is exempt from these orientations, and an especially contagious social development, reliance on racial difference in the formation and development of the country, has saddled the United States with an ugly and tenacious cultural expression of the superiority complex. Racism, as a manifestation of the superiority complex, may individuate, but it also feeds virulent levels of isolation and loneliness in a society.

Within the memory of many still alive, all black Americans were kept in a void so deep as to appear invisible, a status reified in Ralph Ellison's novel *Invisible Man* (1952). Racism eliminated education, vocation, citizenship, law, opportunity, wealth, relation, and often life itself to a large minority living in the country. No degree of reparation or explanation can answer for what has happened or continues to happen in elements of discrimination that remain in place today.

So stark have been basic denials to so many people across the history of the United States that no two individuals coming from opposite sides of racial difference can look at the country in quite the same way, and the act of looking complicates the problems. The most devastating manifestations of racial difference, the horrors of slavery, are only partially retrievable from the darkest hole in American history.

Imagination therefore competes with investigation to recover a past that no one can fully know, and plumbing the price of racial difference in millions of unrecorded lives falls to literature as much as to history. By default, the novel of racial difference has become the uncanny source of repressed knowledge with a problem of its own. How can one fictionalize injustice on such a scale with integrity?

In response to that question, abnormality has become the logical obsession of works that focus on the history of racial difference. The best of the novelists who take up this subject have turned perversion of the home and familial significance into a unique form of tragedy. William Faulkner called *Absalom, Absalom!*, published in 1936, the idea of a man who wanted sons and got sons who destroyed him. Half a century later, in 1987, Toni Morrison constructed her own narrative of the slaveholding South, *Beloved,* around a slave mother who killed her baby to save it from bondage.

Slavery in a free country has spawned generational outrage unheard of on other subjects. *Absalom, Absalom!* presents a twisted creation myth with birthing as a form of destruction. Thomas Sutpen builds a civilization on the backs of slave labor and watches it shatter against the aberrant racism at its familial core. *Beloved* renders the subjugated in that aberration. We move from corruption of the American dream to its imposition as nightmare, and the distance covered is a genealogy of the country's defining sin.

Morrison's black daughters appear in answer to Faulkner's white sons. Dominant patterns in communal thought explain *Absalom, Absalom!* Subjugated consciousness clarifies *Beloved*. Deep in the contrast is the full melancholy of racial thought, with each novelist organizing one side of the chasm in difference. *Absalom, Absalom!* and *Beloved* are companion texts across this divide. They come from either end of racial injustice in America, and like the hands from different people trying to clap, they share attributes as well as the awkward rhythms of an impossible situation.

Gothic fictions of terror with secrets buried in haunted houses, both novels employ unreliable narrators, abrupt rhetorical shifts, buried subplots, sudden interior monologues, and artifactual relics barely deciphered. They insist that a difficult story must be just as difficult for the reader to grasp, and so inner states of mind cross communal understandings in bewildering narrative jumps.

Absalom, Absalom! and *Beloved* also prove that the long half-life of injustice distorts the present as well as the past by jumbling the order of the generations. The domestic scene is filled with malice and distortion. Parents kill their children instead of raising them. Love becomes impossible even with one's closest. Slavery and its aftermath are worse than discrepancies in the national experiment; they destroy its basic unit, the American family. This is the story that Faulkner and Morrison record over the fifty-year span that allows it to be told.

Absalom, Absalom!

No two characters in American fiction create their own isolation quite as stringently as those at the center of Faulkner's story: Thomas Sutpen, the source, and Quentin Compson, the receiver of it. In one of many reversals of the norm for psychological health, their development from loneliness into thoughtful solitude destroys them instead of saving them. Sutpen dies in claimed strength; Quentin, in realized weakness. Faulkner wants no solution for either figure in his account of racism as tragic isolation—an isolation so complete that only in the year 2010 did it come to light that Faulkner's vision of genealogical distortion depends on actual plantation records.

The myth of success in American culture celebrates self-reliance, and Thomas Sutpen is the avatar of that understanding. He embodies "that solitude of contempt and distrust which success brings to him who gained it because he was strong instead of merely lucky." His rise fuels "the ruthless Sutpen code of taking what it wanted provided it was strong enough." Larger than other human lives, Sutpen's also sinks beneath them.

The rigidities of racist thought are at fault, but Sutpen succeeds through more general ideological concerns in the culture. He is, in consequence, a national, not a regional problem. When, as a "forlorn nameless and lost" backcountry boy, he is sent on an errand and denied the right to speak by a black servant at the front door of a tidewater planter's mansion, he cannot believe he has been treated as too inferior to count for anything while doing the man in the mansion a favor.

The boy's reaction to the insult is a reasonable one in a country that presumes to teach "all men are created equal," and it sends him not to the back door, where he is ordered to go, but into his secret hiding place in the woods to think it through. This time, however, solitude undoes the thinker. The ignorant boy is too unconsciously alone in his defining moment to realize what it can mean. He lacks the means to think deeply, and so two countervailing inner voices compete for a simplistic understanding.

Every thought process is mesmerized by the unseen superiority behind the mansion door. One voice argues that the boy must shoot the planter to vindicate his own worth; the other voice, slowly dominant, says no. Instead the rejected boy should answer the insult by becoming the person who rejects others in a mansion of his own, and the effects, based on such a theory, are immediate and far-reaching.

We are watching the superiority complex at work. As one who would be superior, one who can freely insult instead of receiving insult, the boy of fourteen accepts a logical conclusion. His own home and family must be as worthless as the planter assumes. By "tiptoeing out" of the hovel that is no longer a home the next morning without saying a word to anyone, the boy agrees to never see any of his family again; nor, in "turning his back on all he knew," does he ever wish to see them.

The nature of this solution is bizarre only in its sudden conception. Faulkner has given us as concise an illustration of the singularity of purpose and individuality required for success in the American dream as one can find anywhere in the culture. Later, as the successful planter himself, Sutpen logically accepts that rejecting his own son, Charles Bon, replicates the first refusal at the mansion door. Rejection of unworthiness remains the correlative in the assumption of superior worth.

Racial mixing within a racist code gives Sutpen his predicament, but so does the worship of individualism in the land of opportunity and progress. The man who builds his own mansion and plantation by himself believes he can be whatever he wants to be by personal effort, and the same theory means that a man who succeeds should be able to pay away any mistakes that he makes. Success—the American entitlement of those who work hard enough—can erase the past through its own right to advance.

Sutpen accordingly looks for "the mistake" rather than the ethical bind when his white family of wife, son, and daughter unravels over denial of the seemingly white but technically black oldest son from a previous marriage. Charles Bon, Charles the Good, is Sutpen's most accomplished child. He can remain a bosom companion as the unacknowledged brother of son Henry, but the racist code means he can be fiancé to daughter Judith only as long as he is the unconnected white man he appears to be on first arrival.

There is, in fact, no mistake as long as Sutpen's design relies, like that of so many, on the single-minded "way to wealth," a philosophy coined first in America by Benjamin Franklin. The American obsession with prosperity compounds the racial contradiction that makes it possible. The mistake, if we can call it that, is the history of the United States. Faulkner gives the parallel in exact terms: "High morality was concomitant with the money, and the sheen on the dollars was not from gold but from blood."

For a slave-driven prosperity to work, human beings must be broken into tools. Sutpen rules others through his strength, but the moral neutrality required to make others the implements of his success causes him to treat his wife and children the same way. In behavioral terms, the problem is again not limited to slavery; it can be found anywhere in a country where success is the money that defines it.

Faulkner makes Sutpen's design especially crude for another reason. Refinement of distinction hides the inconsistencies in an unjust society. Sutpen is without the veneer of time. He is "underbred," where breeding turns tyranny into the hierarchy of a deserving elite. Alone in his vision but not lonely, Sutpen emerges too suddenly and calmly visible in a society that "agreed never to for-give him for not having a past."

Lack of breeding causes Sutpen to be obtuse to the ceremonies in legitimacy that the town pecking order requires, and his mistakes destroy him; but the central drama of the novel is a matter of planning, not miscal-culation. Sutpen's most appalling decision comes when he embraces his white son and acknowledged heir, Henry, and orders him, through love, to get rid of the unac-knowledged black one.

Faulkner's declared source is the biblical punishment of King David in Second Samuel, a parallel story of in-cest and violence. When David takes the wife of Uriah for his own, after arranging for Uriah's death in battle, God, through the prophet Nathan, answers, "I will raise up evil against thee out of thine own house." A son of David rapes one of his own half sisters, and he is killed by her full brother for it. The murderer, Absalom, Da-vid's favorite son, then rebels against his father and is killed for it, leading to David's lament, "Absalom, my son, my son, Absalom!"

Absalom, Absalom! makes sons "the natural enemy" of their father; they pay for their father's crime "because wasn't it done that way in the old days?" The marriage of Charles Bon and Judith Sutpen is suspended when Sutpen reveals Charles to be the older half-brother from a spurned first marriage, but Sutpen's "trump" is mis-cegenation. Henry Sutpen can accede to incest but not racial difference.

Faulkner uses these incestuous and racial confusions to stage the primal scene of difference in an exchange between Henry and Charles around a wartime campfire. They are exhausted Confederate soldiers in a failed war that complicates the denial they cannot handle:

> —*You are my brother.*
>> —*No I'm not. I'm the nigger that's going to sleep with your sister. Unless you stop me Henry.*

Henry does stop Charles. His decision to murder the unresisting Charles, the older brother whom he emulates and who has saved his life on the battlefield, makes Henry a guilt-ridden, lifelong fugitive, and it ruins the life of their mutual sister Judith. Sutpen, "fog-bound by his own private embattlement of personal morality," has manipulated his children's lives until they destroy one another.

The key to the novel lies in this multilayered confusion over difference in mixed yet estranged generations. The racist animus between begetter and begot pollutes everything: it defeats life, liberty, reason, youth, age, and (most pitifully) intimacy, the shared quality that should thrive in the domestic scene of family life.

The deformation of generational significance exists at every level. The intricacies are as hard to follow as they are ultimately terrifying. Rosa Coldfield, decades younger than her dying sister Ellen, the mother of Judith and Henry, is asked by Ellen to take care of the fully grown Judith even though Rosa, four years younger than Judith, has no skill or means to offer other than the formal office of "aunt." Clytemnestra, the rejected (because black) half sister of Judith, has received the same assignment from Sutpen as her slave companion, though Clytemnestra never once accepts for herself the name of slave.

The three women live together as "three strangers" across racial difference and against the backdrop of the Civil War being fought to force a new level of recognition. Unacknowledged siblings, Judith and Clytemnestra cannot be equals in affection though lifelong companions, while Rosa abjures all thought of the slave "Clytie." The distinctions make them worse than strangers. Rosa and Clytemnestra are *"open, ay honorable, enemies"* in the competition of caring for Judith, who remains oblivious to all such attention as improbable niece, unacknowledged sister, and tacit mistress.

Racism, insisting on difference, perverts passions and creates weapons within the domestic scene. When Charles Bon's orphaned, partially black child Charles Etienne Bon comes to Sutpen's plantation, he must sleep on a cot below the bed of "the cold unbending" Judith and above the pallet on the floor of Clytemnestra, where he absorbs "the fierce ruthless constant guardianship of the negress." Loved by neither, Charles Etienne will throw away his life in "indictment of heaven's ordering."

All these repressed frustrations in difference remain mute and are only fully grasped half a century later in 1910 by Quentin Compson, another boy-man from the South, six years older than Sutpen at the mansion door but as vulnerable to the cultural insult he finds in front of him. Quentin pieces the story together from three sources: the enraged spinster Rosa Coldfield, his cynical father, and finally, his ironic roommate, the Canadian Shreve McCannon, during Quentin's first winter at Harvard College.

For Rosa the story vindicates her life. For Mr. Compson and Shreve it feeds sarcastic byplay. For Quentin, who alone learns the whole story, it turns into a burgeoning source of despair. Despite the shared story with Shreve in their college room, Quentin remains alone in understanding, "panting in the cold air, the iron New England dark." The warm rising bond of teller and listener that heals Isabel Archer and Janie Mae Crawford is nothing but cold, acidic disintegration here.

Quentin lives just far enough from the past to see all of the cruelties that previous generations could hide from themselves in the decorum of a slave culture. He sees the whole truth, and it kills him. Readers of Faulkner's earlier novel, *The Sound and the Fury* (1929), know that Quentin commits suicide at the end of this school year.

The story of Sutpen exposes the absence of all empathy in a world based on difference, and that absence has given Quentin's emotions no room for growth or change. Terribly alone while rethinking the intolerable past in his "flat, curiously dead voice," he is "older at twenty than a lot of people who have died." We have another version of the southern boy looking at the mansion, and this one is dead before he has lived.

Less apparent is the way this second level of tragedy hides a third. The last of Sutpen's ruined children is his half-black, eldest child and daughter, Clytemnestra. She lives as the by-blow from her unacknowledged father's rape of an unnamed slave, and although we never enter her mind, "she is," Faulkner reveals, "the one who owns the terror." As the longest-lived victim of Sutpen's design and named after the bitterest lost figure in Aeschylus's play *The Eumenides,* she is justice denied. All women are pawns in Sutpen's hands, but Clytemnestra is the sterile protector of a legacy that never includes her.

"Clytie," the offspring of a father who rejects the connection and a forgotten mother, disappears within the final conflagration of the Sutpen mansion in 1910. Even here she registers only in white men's conjectures:

> The tragic gnome's face beneath the clean headrag against a red background of fire, seen for a moment between two swirls of smoke, looking down at them, perhaps not even now with triumph and no more of despair than it had ever worn, possibly even serene above the

    melting clapboards before the smoke swirled
    across it again.

If this most tragic face can hide despair, it may be because the owner of it, showing the only thing she owns, has kindled the fire that destroys the design. She has prepared the wood and lit the match. Part of Sutpen's design but held outside of its meaning, she is the last actor in it. If Clytemnestra can be thought to be serene, it may be because she completes the fall of the house of Sutpen.

Beloved

Art notwithstanding, to be burnt alive hurts more than implied serenity will allow. Much of importance is left out of the person that Clytemnestra had to have been, and everything about this picture is reversed in *Beloved* except "the terror." The negative of Faulkner's photograph, rendering black where he sees white, *Beloved* focuses on the enslaved rather than the possessor, on women more than men, on the interior life of the forgotten over the apparent profile of communal leaders, above all, on the misery of those bound instead of the thoughts and actions of those who so unjustly bind.

Like Harriet Beecher Stowe in *Uncle Tom's Cabin,* Toni Morrison begins by proving that a seemingly benevolent slave arrangement is still a revolting contradiction in the domestic scene. The original plantation owner,

Mr. Garner, garners an illegitimate form of wealth. He says he treats his slaves like men and women but names them as a group rather than as individuals, and the lie becomes clear as soon as he dies. As in Stowe's account of Simon Legree, the entrance of an abominable overseer, suitably named "Schoolteacher," instructs everyone in the cruelty of being owned by another.

But if more horrifying in the physical details it conveys than *Absalom, Absalom!* Morrison's *Beloved* is curiously optimistic in comparison. There may be a lesson in the contrast: those who have controlled life, the slave-owning South, become more philosophically pessimistic than those who are just getting the chance to try. Aspirations work better than attrition in the often ruthless business of existence.

Morrison's lovers, Sethe and Paul D, have faced devastating torments and losses that break their self-esteem in slavery. Even when technically free, they have too much to fear from racial difference around them, and they are separated from each other by personal degradation and betrayal. Nevertheless, their reconciliation at novel's end takes place over a future felt to be available. "Me and you got more yesterday than anybody," Paul D tells Sethe. "We need some kind of tomorrow."

Undone and alone by all she has been through, Sethe begins to recover through Paul D's act of sympathy and love. "You your best thing, Sethe. You are," Paul D concludes, reaching out to her. Domestic love is about relation, placement, acceptance, respect, the end of isolation, or, as Paul D learns, it is about taking the splintered pieces and putting them "in all the right order," an act of intellect as well as emotion. Sethe responds to his appeal with a question for more contact when she answers, "Me? Me?"

Morrison writes of the tenacity that survival requires. Her story, based loosely on historical events, recounts a fugitive slave mother's precarious existence after she has murdered her own baby girl to prevent its return to slavery. The unspeakable crime is an assertion against the equally unspeakable degradation in slavery. So honest is this tainted affirmation at the expense of another that only the ghost of the murdered child has the right to challenge what the mother has done to her, and in that challenge Sethe's tenuous commitment to life is one of two strands in the novel.

Sethe's life is tenuous because love is dangerous as well as a resource. One strategy in slavery says, "Don't love nothing." You cannot lose when the person taken has never been yours to lose. Yet not caring destroys too. Absence of love, as in Faulkner's novel, brings a loneliness too terrible to bear. *Beloved* responds with the claim of relationship. The free will in love defines liberty: "to get to a place where you could love anything you chose—not to need permission for desire—well now, *that* was freedom."

Negation dominates a first reading of Morrison's novel. Slaves have limbs amputated. They are burned alive, hanged, decapitated, yoked, mouthed with bits,

raped, starved, forced to give a mother's milk for a master's pleasure, made to beg for food, scourged to the
point of disfigurement, and constantly humiliated.
Sethe summarizes slavery: "Anybody white could take
your whole self for anything that came to mind. Not
just work, kill, or maim you, but dirty you . . . so bad
you forgot who you were."

Morrison tries to convey "the unspeakable things, unspoken" in slavery and its aftermath, Reconstruction.
She reaches for the forgotten in history. In *Absalom, Absalom!* the field slaves flee Sutpen's plantation in the Civil
War. They seem to melt away, disappearing in fact as
well as narrative. *Beloved* recovers the missing person
that had to exist somewhere inside the named runaway.

A runaway, by definition, needs somewhere to run to.
Where did the slave, or the suddenly emancipated person, *go,* out of the enforced ignorance of a life less than
life because without choice? Morrison writes, "You
couldn't run if you didn't know how to go," and if you
went anyway, "you could be lost forever."

Much of *Beloved* is about those lost forever. We see the
power in this priority when Morrison characterizes the
black diaspora of the 1860s in all its massive, unavoidable, unaided aimlessness:

> During, before and after the War he [Paul D]
> had seen Negroes so stunned, or hungry, or
> tired or bereft it was a wonder they recalled or
> said anything. Who, like him, had hidden in

caves and fought owls for food; who, like him,
stole from pigs; who, like him, slept in trees in
the day and walked by night; who, like him, had
buried themselves in slop and jumped in wells
to avoid regulators, raiders, patrollers, veterans,
hill men, posses, and merry makers.

To be so much as "found" as a black vagrant could be
fatal. Paul D, a survivor on the run, tells the story of "a
witless colored woman jailed and hanged for stealing
ducks she believed were her own babies." He conveys the
strategies of a huge population too lost to be remembered: "Move. Walk. Run. Hide. Steal and move on."
Hiding counts as success, but succeeding means you
remain lost. For if you were strong enough, fortunate
enough, and clever enough to remain concealed, you remained out of the history being told.

Can there be a greater loneliness than to be on the
run with nothing, nowhere to go, no one to trust, no
one to help, and no one to care or remember whether
you live or die? The resourcefulness necessary to survive
made the runaway an unavoidable thief and hence a
mutual danger in every act of discovery. Morrison tells
this story in a way that no reader can forget. It may be
the greatest power in a novel that crosses over into the
history that cannot be told in any other way.

Beloved works through parallels. Collective examples
of a people oppressed, like the diaspora of slaves on the

run, appear alongside developing characters in a sequential plot. Morrison writes at her best when the conflation of these strands details how the enslaved had to think about impossible situations.

The conflation itself—the hideous facts and scale of slavery against the individuals who outlive it—means that the ability to affirm exists only at an elemental level. In his darkest moment, Paul D turns to his friend Stamp Paid; the name signifies a new identity earned in freedom. Paul wonders how much more must he take, and the answer of Stamp Paid is, "All he can." "All he can."

Resolving to live *all one can* under such circumstances is its own form of heroism. Even in total defeat one must hold to the relations that slavery denies at every turn. In the most courageous example of this determination, Sixto, Paul D's half brother, sings the name of the unborn child his woman carries in her body on her way to freedom as he is caught and burned alive for running away.

The symbol of what freedom might mean to one who doesn't have it is an absent presence in the novel, a character we hear of but never from. The best of the slave brothers, the one that Sethe chooses for her mate on the Garner plantation, is Halle, who buys the freedom of his mother, Baby Suggs, and plans the escape of Sethe, losing his own life in the process. Halle is the best of Baby Suggs's children. "Too good for this world," he has sacrificed himself for something higher. He is love insisting on enduring kinship, the thing taken away from a slave as the fungible property of another.

Morrison's most ambiguous formulation of love supplies the starkest conflation of levels, and it is her boldest stroke: the eponymous character "Beloved." Like all ghosts, this one disturbs the living. Beloved is the murdered child of Sethe come to haunt the mother who killed her. She is the survivor of the Middle Passage. She is every black woman raped by a white master. She is the homeless vagrant, and the totality of all rejected people, so named in an epigraph from the Book of Romans ("I will call them my people, which were not my people, and her beloved, which was not beloved").

Beloved is the past not to be forgotten by anyone who wants to forget. Her abnormality in a novel of abnormalities is clear at once. She enters the novel walking as a fully dressed woman out of water with the "new skin" of the baby who was murdered. She appears just as Paul D, Sethe, and Sethe's daughter Denver return from a day of familial happiness, the first full day on which slavery has been forgotten. Beloved will not be left out. She must come first. The past is always going to be now.

Denver, the future, revels in this new-found "sister" until she realizes "it was a greedy ghost" overwhelming everything in the memories it demands. Sethe falls primary victim to this figure out of the past. She must "make up" for the murder of her child, but atonement for such an act is impossible, and the ghost of the child takes over her life. Beloved possesses Sethe, seduces Paul D, and destroys the family unit.

As the future and the only figure who has grown up in a secure home, Denver alone has the capacity and self-confidence to reach outward. Her contact with neighboring communities leads them to help purge Beloved from the house that can only become a home again when the ghost of the past is removed. The dual nature of this search for normalcy is instructive. It can only happen when individual and communal understandings cohere. We see again Morrison's use of parallels: the personal lives of her characters must somehow overcome the larger historical horrors imposed by racial difference.

Denver's growth from a selfish child into a thoughtful, active young woman coping through the help of others reflects the hope of a newly freed people who seek a responsible present out of an unworkable past. Cooperation is a form of communal love in slowly evolving signs of renewal.

At another level, Beloved can never go away. The ghost ends the novel. She last appears as a homeless, abandoned pregnant black girl leaving bare footprints that "come and go, come and go" in the tall grass. They are footprints a child could fill. There can be no greater image of despair and vulnerability in the postbellum American South than this one of a pregnant diminutive black girl, no more than a child herself, on the run with nowhere to go and no one to help her.

This last appearance of Beloved resonates with the mesmerizing runaway sections of Morrison's story. Beloved is both an individual character and all of slavery. To underline the horror and aimless wandering, Morrison writes it is "not a story to pass on," repeating the phrase three times—but that is exactly what she does. She passes on the lost stories of destroyed lives that some do not wish to recover, that others cannot bear to remember, that a few have tried to reconstruct, and that no American should ever deny.

Yes, it can happen here, and it did. *Beloved,* like its companion text *Absalom, Absalom!,* gives dramatic meaning to the usable in an unusable past. Both novels end with an abandoned, homeless black person moving alone and invisible in the woods. Morrison's pregnant black girl reminds us of Jim Bond, the stunted fugitive black remnant of the Sutpen line. But if Morrison's and Faulkner's last solitary figures seem helpless, handicapped, and unrelated to anyone, they are nonetheless mysteriously empowered.

Beloved and Jim Bond are hidden in these final scenes. We do not know where they are or what they think. Instead, the possibility of thought exists in the invisibility of the solitary figure. These injured, wronged, lonely, abandoned, feared, and resisted victims of discrimination and injustice have power because they elude and evade every attempt to be caught or held in place.

Robbed of all kinship and connection to history, the two timeless, totally isolated fugitives have a permanently separate meaning over everyone and everything around them. The relevance of solitude is uncomfortable and different here, but it is still keyed to reflection. It symbolizes what the country did to itself and can never undo.

8

SAUL BELLOW OBSERVES OLD AGE

The nation was once called "an early republic." Is it now a middle republic? A late republic? Americans live under the oldest constitution of modern times. Back in 1928, Gertrude Stein called the United States "just now the oldest country in the world," and in keeping with the claim, the country's population is older today than it has ever been. Two percent of its people were sixty-five years of age or older in the early republic; as late as 1950 the percentage stood at 8 percent; the count is now over 13 percent and climbing fast. "Gerontification" is the newest anxiety in America.

Novels naturally thrive on communal anxiety, and so it is that venerable spectators watch over the fads and foibles of their culture in current literary vogue. These observers remember the past, question the present, and regret the future with death as a background subject. They often succeed at the expense of the young, and if death comes, it comes on their terms and never in an old age home. Novels in this category recall the storyteller's obsession with age back when the nation could think of itself as young. Silence Dogood, Rip Van Winkle, Natty Bumppo, Clifford Pyncheon, and a host of others live again in spirit. Is it nostalgia or a larger regret that has so many writers turning to venerable heroes and heroines?

Certainly the elder novel, as it might be called, is popular today. Leading examples, starting in the 1950s, include Hemingway's *Across the River and into the Trees* (1950) and *The Old Man and the Sea* (1952), Wallace Stegner's *All the Little Live Things* (1967) and *Angle of Repose* (1971), Robert Penn Warren's *A Place to Come To* (1977), and more recently, any of a number of Philip Roth's novels, including *American Pastoral* (1997), *The Dying Animal* (2001), *Everyman* (2006), and *The Humbling* (2009), Don DeLillo's *White Noise* (1985), and Peter Pouncey's *Rules for Old Men Waiting* (2005). Penelope Fitzgerald's *The Bookshop* (1978) and Penelope Lively's *Moon Tiger* (1987) offer female versions of the form.

The master of the genre, with a number of entries—including *Mr. Sammler's Planet* (1970), *Humboldt's Gift* (1975), *The Dean's December* (1982), and *More Die of Heartbreak* (1987)—is Saul Bellow, who won the Nobel Prize in 1976 in part for the first two novels mentioned.

Mr. Sammler's Planet is, in fact, the archetypical elder novel. It thrives on the generational divide between young and old in a deft mixture of despair, solitude, and wish fulfillment.

In an eerie reprise of earlier fascinations, Artur Sammler, a Polish-Jewish immigrant on the Upper West Side of Manhattan in the troubled spring of 1969, resembles our first hero in American fiction, that other old man, Rip Van Winkle. Both characters are plunged into life-changing difficulty through their wives. When stripped of those wives through no fault of their own, and of all other meaningful contemporaries, both men manage to rise as if from the dead to counsel the young. Revitalized, they achieve new reputations and bring wise counsel to worlds different from anything they previously knew.

Just like Rip, Artur has been set free of all material and bodily worries and saved by relatives who might just as easily have ignored him; and like Rip again, he shapes a new life story out of his tragic past. Both characters are qualified optimists who have overcome looming threats from their communities. If these authorial affinities are systemic rather than calculated, they still apply.

Saul Bellow, like Washington Irving, writes a fantasy of old age. Consider the following. Artur Sammler, a Holocaust victim executed and buried, rises from the mass grave that also contains his wife, and, as a member of the resistance, gets to kill one of his Nazi persecutors.

Destitute in a displaced persons camp at the end of the war, he and his helpless daughter are brought to America by a distant half nephew, Dr. Arnold Elya Gruner, who offers provision, a new home, and status as an honored sage in a new family circle. Dr. Gruner even supplies funds for research and travel.

What elderly, war-ravaged immigrant in the late 1940s could have asked for more? In Bellow's story, wish fulfillment turns into what old age should be but rarely becomes. The novel is full of trouble, as every novel must be, but each crisis ends with Mr. Sammler, a man in his late seventies, on top of the situation and holding forth eloquently on the meaning of what has just transpired and been answered.

Here is a partial list of ills endured and overcome. In two days, Sammler is *physically* threatened by a huge black mugger and pickpocket, *intellectually* threatened by radicals who shout him down as an empty old man at Columbia University, *legally* threatened by a police investigation when his daughter steals a manuscript for him from a guest lecturer at the university, and *economically* and *socially* threatened when his benefactor, Elya Gruner, dies in a hospital of a bursting aneurysm.

Beset on all sides, Sammler conquers all. The pickpocket who humiliated him is savagely beaten before his eyes. The best intellectuals recognize Sammler's worth and celebrate it. The angry owner of the purloined manuscript quickly becomes Sammler's admiring auditor when they meet. Death, to be sure, cannot be conquered, but even here there is ascendance. Sammler is the only relative the dying Dr. Gruner wishes to see, and he is the one to mourn in benediction over Gruner's body at novel's end.

A score of more cerebral victories completes the picture. Sammler quietly wins every argument, and his cogency causes all lesser parties to seek advice over their messed-up lives. The young are especially enamored and arrive full of confession. Whether as wise counselor or supreme interlocutor, Sammler has the learned disquisition or quick answer as required. The unlimited scope of this fantasy becomes clear to any reader of a good newspaper. Mr. Sammler instantly provides the right word when challenged with an arcane clue from a crossword puzzle in the *New York Times*.

Although age is not without its difficulties in *Mr. Sammler's Planet,* its natural wisdom protects our hero from equally natural enemies: namely, decay and illness. Sammler notes "the old always fear they have decayed unaware," but he immediately refutes any personal application with a brilliant flow of insights on the course of human history. All of philosophy remains "*terra cognita* to old Sammler." Wide reading in several languages, with special attention to Latin (shades of Cicero and Seneca), give him the discipline to reach the prized goal of age, an order within oneself.

Physical details correspond to mental acumen. Health is no issue despite age, a difficult life, and a ruined eye from a Nazi rifle butt. Sammler is tireless, flexible, and quick of step for one deep into his eighth decade. He remains handsome enough to attract "elderly widows," and his social skills reveal a polished gentleman whose curiosity about life remains gracefully and energetically intact.

To summarize, Mr. Sammler comes to us as the very paragon of good oldness, exactly what any reader would hope for mentally and physically if fortunate enough to reach the same age. Decay is in the air, but it has nothing to do with Artur Sammler except in prospect. There is, however, a glaring exception in this overly sympathetic picture, and it takes control as one characteristic of the elder novel.

Bellow arranges his story around conflict between the generations, with his protagonist siding decisively with his own set. Virtue, respect, courtesy, decorum, comprehension, wisdom, and direction belong exclusively to the old men in the story. Sammler, the dying Gruner, and (down the social ladder) Dr. Gruner's aging chauffeur, Emil, all possess a superior sense of mission, tact, taste, generosity, and tolerance over the younger generation. They alone serve others by holding themselves to "self-severity."

Bellow loads every balance in favor of these seniors. Only they recognize what happens in a story dominated by the unseemly antics of the young. "We old guys have to go along," regrets the least of them, Emil the chauffeur, deploring the selfish disregard of Gruner's children toward his dying employer. Control through experience,

lots of experience, gives each of these old men philosophical heft. "Words are for the elderly," Sammler explains, "or for the young who are old-in-heart." No one
who is young in the novel comes even close to being
old-in-heart.

Against these virtues, the young are without discipline and control. They are uniformly foolish, scatter-
brained, and selfish. Sammler's daughter, Shula, has
turned into a delusional bag lady on the Upper West
Side. She is "a praying nut" in several religions and sometimes "a lunatic." Dr. Gruner's eldest child, Angela, is a
manipulative sexpot who thinks only about her dying
father's money. His son, Wallace, "a high-I.Q. moron,"
flits from one ruinous scheme to another in rebellion
against his father's success. Dr. Gruner's wealth, which
both children squander, is their only concern.

Lesser figures are even worse. Lionel Feffer, a professor
in his thirties at Columbia University, is a hustler and
sexual predator. He abuses his authority and fails to
meet basic obligations while covering failures in "a bro-
cade of boasts." Margotte Arkin, Sammler's niece and
landlady, is a tedious know-it-all who knows nothing.
Like so many of the young in this book, she is sloppy, in-
effective, and a little unclean, "a bothersome creature"
who "forgot to flush the toilet." Angela's boyfriend,
Wharton Horricker, is consumed by "self-pampering
fastidiousness."

The list of the undeserving goes on and on. Sammler's ex-son-in-law, Eisen, is a maniac who has abused

his former wife. An artist without talent, Eisen tries to sell his awful portraits of Elya Gruner to the dying man in his hospital bed. Dr. Gruner's own doctor, also young, gives more time to betting pools on sports than his patient's condition. Every negative twist in plot begins with the irresponsible young. There is not a single younger person in the novel that we are asked to like, much less respect.

A perceptive witness, Sammler quietly exposes youth as it ignores the common sense he offers only when asked. He dismisses the young around him and is overly clinical toward the relation closest to him, his "woman-lunatic" of a daughter. "Sammler knew her ways, knew them as the Eskimo knows the ways of the seal."

Bellow makes this one-sided conflict believable by tying it to the disintegration of life in New York City. There are dog-fouled, garbage-strewn sidewalks, busted phone booths used as urinals, condemned buildings covered with graffiti, parks that are dangerous rather than beautiful, unaddressed crime and the indifference of authority to it. Elements of urban decline are sprinkled throughout the novel and represent "the suicidal impulses of civilization." America, once young, appears to be aging fast, and although "youth is big business," its "sovereign youth-style" looks ridiculous when every tie to progress is cut off from it.

Severe critic though he may be, Sammler personally avoids the vortices of anger and disgust that exist between the generations, and he does so by manifesting the best qualities of youth! Sammler is invariably curious about what is happening around him and never jaded in his reactions. He likes slang and has learned "to divert himself with perceptions." "When he went out, life was not empty." Until very recently, he has even managed to join the young running in Riverside Park!

This is the regime of a younger man couched within the wisdom of an older one. Sammler's personal disaster in the Holocaust has taught him how easily the human spirit can be twisted, and it has knocked all false pride and social pretension out of him. In control of his own vanities and foibles, he identifies them in others with devastating accuracy. "You had to be able to bear the tangles of the soul, the sight of cruel dissolution," Sammler reminds himself during one moment of crisis.

The word "Sammler" means "collector" or "gatherer" in Yiddish, and the collector in this case charts up the pluses and minuses with no illusions about "the slackness, the cowardice of the world." Yes, "things are falling apart," and life suggests "a state of singular dirty misery," literally "a terror," but Sammler rejects such "poverty of soul" and lives "with a civil heart" in "archetypes of goodness."

Bellow, like so many American writers, insists on an innate goodness against the odds, even though Artur has endured the worst. Dismissed as a human being by his Nazi executioners and saved by blind chance from the mass grave in Cracow that absorbs all others, Sammler still believes "there is the same truth in the heart of every human being . . . the richest thing we share in common." He even hopes that a glance between enemies can save, though he has to admit that he enjoyed the act of killing just such an enemy.

Of course, the good wise man can only be a perceptive witness if he also acknowledges the bad. *Mr. Sammler's Planet* solves the problem through juxtapositions. "Man is a killer. Man has a moral nature," Sammler observes, speaking somewhat of himself. How, then, is one to behave in a fallen world? The useful spectator keeps his balance by "translating heartache into delicate, even piercing observation." Such balance is not achieved without struggle. Against "a terrible dumbness," "compassionate utterance is a mortal necessity." No matter the situation before us, "signs could be made, should be made, must be made." We die or kill each other. "Nevertheless, there is a bond. There is a bond."

Some slippage in the novel occurs here. Clinical observation vies repeatedly with a more active sympathy. Despite the claim of a human bond, Sammler remains an outsider in habitual detachment. He is seemingly close to real identifications, and yet not really there: "He, personally, stood aside from all developments." Even before the Holocaust, the younger Artur has freed himself of relations. An Anglicized Jew in an Englishman's hat, Sammler has never been interested in his Polish forebears, and he has to admit that he lives now "somewhat separated from the rest of the species."

The idea of death increases the thinker's perception but also his distance from others. In his late seventies, Sammler knows he exists in "one of those penultimate springs," and for once erudition is not enough, even in reflection. He confesses that "the inward, the intimate, the dear life—the thing that is oneself from earliest days— when it first learns of death is often crazed." Crazed or worse. Can we call upon our "best qualities" when the time comes? Sammler has his doubts. "That was all very well," he decides, "until death turned its full gaze on the individual. Then all such ideas were as nothing." Like Pascal introducing *Pensées,* he believes "there is noth- ing more real than that, or more terrible."

Sammler struggles with the idea of death. It perco- lates throughout his ruminations. "Humankind could not endure futurelessness," and yet "death was the sole visible future," a fact few acknowledge and all hide from. With astronauts landing on the moon, Sammler is amused by those who sublimate their fears in the hope of escape to it. The superficial meaning of the title, *Mr. Sammler's Planet,* lies here in Artur's acceptance of his fate. He exists trapped in "this death-burdened, rotting, spoiled, sullied, exasperating, sinful earth."

The thought is its own loneliness. Artur Sammler has already been through the imagined moment of death while digging his own grave in Cracow under gunpoint, and the experience has led to "preoccupation with the subject, the dying, the mystery of dying, the state of death." Stripped in Cracow of the previous generation and his own, he has made no spiritual connection with the next and says he does "not much mind his oblivion, not with such as would do the remembering, anyway."

Of course, he does mind. Who would not like to be remembered? Sammler, alas, finds no younger living person to admire or even respect on intellectual terms, and so he gives up the wish. The dead are helpless in the memory of the living, and Sammler accepts that no one after will even want to get it right about him. Extreme solitude becomes its own problem here. Sammler's only emotional link at the end of the novel is to the dead, to Elya Gruner, who lies before him in the postmortem room of the hospital. Here, in short, are the manifest problems of old age. The novel is about how to be equal to them.

Whatever remains of solace in life sounds somewhat legalistic in Bellow's hero. Looking down at the dead man who knew he was dying, Sammler decides that the good thing about Dr. Gruner, and presumably about himself, is that "he did meet the terms of his contract." The loneliness in this statement is palpable. Bellow has gone to great lengths in *Mr. Sammler's Planet* to prove that no one in the younger generation thinks in terms of life's contract or cares what it might mean to fulfill one.

Artur Sammler has known tragedy and overcome it. He is a sympathetic observer with a critical bite. He looks for the best in people but records the worst. He is an educated intellectual in a world of ignorance and prejudice. He is a wise elder looking askance at those around him and at what is coming after him. Most of all, he is alone in a wicked world that will have no reason to miss him. Can any of these disparities work for him?

The polarities come together in the reported deterioration of American culture. The clarity of the elderly spectator poised on the upside of his own dissolution (and in fear of it) gives him a knowing perspective on the decline all around him. Bellow's use of the disparity is constant and has a higher purpose. Sammler, who should be in terrible health from worldly knocks, is in great shape, while America, which has no reason to crumble, seems to be falling down all around him.

The contrast in health between the self and deterioration in society keys Bellow's nuanced satire of age and decay. The novel is a protest against national decline eased just enough by the erudition, equanimity, wry humor, and ironic perspective that Artur Sammler's sophistication brings to it.

Bellow's America remains comic in the sense that it is "staggering, if not breaking." If the nation should be enjoying "the wisdom born of prolongation," as Sammler is doing, it has abandoned the opportunity to pursue instead "erotic, Roman voodoo primitivism." The country has lost direction and thus significance in the eyes of one capable of gauging its meaning. "In America," Bellow has Sammler observing, "certain forms of success required an element of parody, self-mockery, a satire on the-thing-itself."

The list of recorded ills is as familiar as it is long. Consumer prosperity has left the country without majestic aspirations; the integrity of its fabric has become vulnerable to "the stupidities of power" and "the fraudulence of business." Self-indulgence rather than service dominates the gauge of the citizen ("everything is poured so barbarously and recklessly into personal gesture"). The noble experiment in democratic living is now "to each according to his excitability."

By the same token, the novel is not a screed. Bellow is a master at protecting his observer from his own authorial cynicism. He has Mr. Sammler admit to a certain excitement over America: "The charm, the ebullient glamour, the almost unbearable agitation that came from being able to describe oneself as a twentieth-century American was available to all." There are "fascinating opportunities for the mind and the soul." Then again, are they really available to all? Sammler has his doubts: "a man would have to be unusually intelligent," "unusually nimble and discerning," to comprehend what mass inclusion in America portends. Fortunately, Sammler is unusually intelligent, as well as nimble and discerning!

As an inhabitant of America for twenty-two years, Mr. Sammler finds himself caught between levels of insight. In intellectual terms, he is at once a separate elitist in comprehension and the reassuring democrat who wants to belong. Bellow, in recognition, has deprived Sammler of sight in one eye. His protagonist thus sees with "two different-looking eyes," one outward and the other inward.

Whenever a novelist divides perception in a protagonist this way, the reader should take notice. "One eye is functioning," Sammler reports in jocular fashion, in case the point is missed. "Like the old saying about the one-eyed being King in the Country of the Blind." To take this joke as deliberately as it is delivered, we must ask what should this "King" be doing? Is he the knowing clinician who dissects, or the sympathetic observer who reaches out in appreciation with some hope of helping those around him?

Bellow himself seems torn over the possibilities. He implies that only an individual separated from the herd can grasp a deeper purpose in things, but Sammler in that role raises troubling worries. "Where is the desirable self that one might be?" he wonders, looking inward. Is more than personal soul-searching required of this philosophe steeped in the learning of the modern world as well as the classical tradition? Can the man who has developed a working solitude make it work for others?

Matters are understandably different when the eye turns outward onto the streets of New York, but hardly better. The flâneur as sympathetic observer fastens all too quickly on the lowest possible common denominator: "the Woolworth store, cheap tin or plastic from the five-and-dime of souls." "Seeing it this way," Sammler ponders, "a man may feel that being human is hardly worth the trouble."

The stance is alarming in one already detached, and the real unanswered tension in the novel takes hold here. The pressure of wanting a democratic bond annoys the solitary thinker by projecting him into social complications. Most characters in the novel seek out Mr. Sammler because they think he has "some unusual power, magical perhaps, to affirm the human bond." He is thinking man, and they are not, but his capacity to affirm the human bond is demonstrably weak. The presence of others in Sammler's life interrupts serious thought only long enough for the expert to record their failures. In effect, Bellow's social satire, with Mr. Sammler as its clinical vehicle, gets in the way of the character study, the philosophically adept helping hand at the center of the novel.

Sammler listens to the problems brought to him but always with a distaste that is closest to his real nature. In the one moment when he turns writer himself, his letter of apology to Professor Lal over his daughter's theft of Lal's manuscript, he reveals his predicament. How does one match intellectual perception (aloof and critical) with belonging (the balms of connection)? Artur's personal struggle for place is instructive: "Everyone grapples, each in his awkward muffled way, with a power, a Jacob's angel, to get a final satisfaction or glory that is withheld."

For Sammler, final satisfaction lies in thought, but to what end, particularly since that priority seems to limit the power of sympathy in him? Bellow shows his awareness by constantly trapping his protagonist *in media res*. Narrow temporal needs, the tedious problems in everyday life, lead to confusion of purpose. There is "unfinished business" to be performed, but Sammler wonders "how did business finish?" "We entered in the middle of things," he reasons, "and somehow become convinced that we must conclude it." But as he says to himself, "How?" A survivor, "was he meant to do something?"

In the end, Sammler can only claim that everyone knows or should know "the terms of his contract" against "all the confusion and degraded clowning of this life through which we are speeding." A vague idea of assignments reinforces his belief in social bonding and contract. "We have our assignments," he tells the wrong person, the inattentive and impatient Angela Gruner, as her father Elya Gruner dies; their stipulations are "feeling, outgoingness, expressiveness, kindness, heart."

These are fine words, even if the implication of their absence outrages the selfish Angela, but where do they lead? Who decides when business is finished? Who sets the terms of the contract? Who makes the assignments? What is the extent of kindness? How do the heartless find a heart? Sammler's fortifying vocabularies of business and law lack feeling and direction. They express the role of obligation in bloodless terms. Sammler's age in "the eighth decade of one's life" releases him from the active life, but he dissects more than he feels, and he reacts more than he initiates.

Bellow protects this reactive stance in the same way Irving protects Rip Van Winkle. Perception can trump emotional engagement because perception is the worthier gauge late in life. Even so, distance is what we notice in Sammler's thought on relations. Just listen to him: "A family, a circle of friends, a team of the living got things going, and then death appeared and no one was prepared to acknowledge death." The idea of death again separates the thinker from those around him. Here again are some of the confusions in old age when domestic possibilities and human relations dwindle.

One of Bellow's solutions is an unlikely active life in his elderly protagonist. Sammler, comfortable alone, is rarely actually alone in this novel. He has been given a busy social agenda of needy others that comports with the fantasy of worth in elder novels. The solution seems to be to have it all without wanting it. Preferring solitude, Sammler finds few worthy of engagement and treats those so constantly on his doorstep with an ascendant alienation or even dismissal as the privilege that age allows itself. Bellow's philosopher is important to his thought; the social man is important to his story.

At other points Bellow speaks another way. He says his protagonist is "a sad old man" in whom "affections had been consumed." Sammler's "one time precious life had been burnt away," and now there are "no rapid connections" or "spontaneous feeling of friendship" left.

When Elya Gruner dies, Bellow's hero comes close to fatalistic decrepitude. He mourns a larger continuum of loss familiar in the old, "deprived of one more thing, stripped of one more creature. One more reason to live trickled out."

If there is a delusion in Bellow's use of the elder novel it lies in this use of it. His hero is at once an engaged participant and a wise man in knowing retreat. Sammler must wear a two-faced mask to guide events as well as the novel of ideas. There is the willing village elder and then the silent perceiver. In plot terms Bellow does not know quite what to do with the tension he has created between effective association and a saving solitude, and the excuse of age often covers the difference.

Artur Sammler, uneasy on his planet, stands for the proposition that a serious thinker in America will spend a great deal of time alone. But again to what end? Is the candle, in this case Sammler's austere assessment of others, worth the price? The question carries beyond fiction. Is "Artur"—a remarkably preserved, young older man out of "Author"—a realistic answer to the problem of decay or the wish-fulfillment of a novelist who cannot quite face the reality of what old age brings?

On the other hand, age is about these very ambivalences, and the power in solitude offered here is not without grit in dealing with them. To know one's contract is also to intuit one's life story as it is happening and to settle something of the purpose behind it so that recognition continues to build.

We see as much in perhaps the most distressing moment for the intellectual in the novel. We are in the age of youthful rebellion, and when a packed house of students shouts him down as he lectures at Columbia University, Sammler at first rails in thought against them, but he quickly recovers by reminding himself "a human being, valuing himself for the right reasons," must first make sure that "the internal parts are in order." These observations are well taken in any crisis. The wise observer has rescued the participant in a moment of need.

There is a proper temperament in a crisis of "both knowing and not knowing—one of the more frequent human arrangements," Sammler observes while analyzing the predicament of the dying Elya Gruner. The sick man, a doctor himself, knows he has been "summoned to the brink of the black." How is he to come to terms personally with that realization in the hospital bed that he knows he will never leave?

To be human is to arrange things for oneself in proportion to what is possible. Always precise especially in the presence of death, Sammler is against "seeing the singular human creature demand more when the sum of human facts could not yield more." A precise acquaintance with the sum of available human facts is itself important and its own answer against retreat and disengagement.

Thus and despite its flaws, *Mr. Sammler's Planet* is peculiarly valuable for its portrayal of a tenacity in thought and the courage that goes with it. There is a lesson to be wrung from age itself. The more one has seen, the greater the desire should be to arrange what has happened. "To compose our character is our duty," Montaigne insists in "On Experience." Bellow argues that this duty becomes more significant as we move along. It is the resource against everything that might drag us down.

9

DON DELILLO AND MARILYNNE ROBINSON
MOURN LOSS

Paradise Lost, the great epic on the subject, resists return after loss. Those who survive can only go forward. Anyone who lives long enough also absorbs Shakespeare's "fearful meditation" in Sonnet 65. Time, "the wrackful siege of battering days," takes from us in every conceivable way. "Where, alack, shall Time's best jewel from Time's chest lie hid?" the poet asks, and he answers "O, none."

How often can we adjust to what the days take away? What does repeated loss do to us? But we do adjust no matter what it does, that being the way of things, and we do it in one of two ways. We cope through the animal needs of reaction that define us or through the measure of our humanity.

Two contemporary novels address the problem from these polar directions. In Don DeLillo's *Falling Man* from 2007, Keith Neudecker, an alienated New York lawyer already separated from home and family, falls into deeper estrangement and permanent trauma. He enters the pages of the novel as a wounded animal, and he remains one. He is "organic shrapnel," "a man scaled in ash, in pulverized matter," stumbling away from the twin towers on September 11, 2001, while friends die trapped inside.

Marilynne Robinson's *Gilead* from 2004 offers a contrast in every way but one. The Reverend John Ames embraces what he does with purpose, and he has found domestic happiness after many years alone, but at seventy-six, he suffers from a fatal aneurysm that will kill him at any moment. Neudecker's life is a splintering mess; Ames's dwindling days reach for the holistic wonders in existence.

At first glance, the isolating despair and secularity of *Falling Man* seem completely distinct from the thirst for life and religious invocations of *Gilead,* but only at first glance. The untimely death of many people horrifies us, but natural death from illness presents a comparable dilemma. Arguably, it is the same dilemma: mortality facing itself. There are differences, but both men engage with loss alone.

Each character's way of coping also tells us something about human nature in extremity. Keith Neudecker, hermetically enclosed and withholding, shrinks within the jumble of narrative snippets that make up *Falling Man.*

John Ames struggles expansively to convey the coherence of his life as it closes in *Gilead*. DeLillo mixes many voices without warning. We constantly check to realize who is speaking. Robinson gives us a single undifferentiated, sometimes droning voice in an unending monologue meant for the six-year-old son who might never read the mound of words that will be left behind.

The silent man traumatized by public catastrophe in *Falling Man* has the same problem of ultimate meaning as his garrulous counterpart in the privacy of *Gilead*. To witness the sudden death of many people arrests the soul, but what of a life that passes unremembered for what it saw of value? How many lives end without their realization noted? Does collective devastation reduce the problem in what is always a solitary end?

DeLillo and Robinson bring radically different resources and normative concerns to these questions, and yet they rely on parallel lines of force to tell their stories. Both novelists deploy the simplest of nuclear families: a wife, a husband, and a very young male child too young to understand. The promises of connection remain unfulfilled even in these spare, smallest of intimate family circles. The characters in both novels have trouble talking to others about what is important to all of them.

The silences in these decidedly separate lives are instructive and produce similar themes. Both novelists insist on the starkest of separations between the generations. Both assume that the contemplation of loss is a lonely pursuit. Both project the trauma in their fictional families onto a vexed template of modernity.

DeLillo and Robinson also find many of the same problems in their vastly different views of the country. All their characters are anxious about change, fearful of aging, and consumed by communal disintegration. The paranoia and aimlessness of upper-middle-class New Yorkers in *Falling Man* match the depression over deteriorating physical conditions in the Midwestern village of *Gilead*.

Nothing is quite right for anyone in either setting. DeLillo's characters are full of anger, fear, resentment, and occasional violence in their proximity to the rubble from 9/11. They look for more planes flying into buildings and more people falling out of them. Robinson sets her village in rural Iowa, where farming no longer prospers. The young leave Gilead as soon as they can. The biblical name "Gilead" means "hard" or "barren." It is where King David goes to grieve over the death of his son Absalom, and Robinson is attuned. She builds her own version of Gilead around rebellious sons.

The mental equipment differs so greatly in these two novels from the twenty-first century that we must not forget their commonalities. DeLillo and Robinson give us Americans who seem to belong to different countries in much the way John Dos Passos shocks his readers at the end of *The Big Country* (1936) by grimly announcing, "All right we are two countries," but there is less shock in the premise today. Symptomatic of larger conflicts,

DeLillo's coastal and urban secularists and Robinson's Midwestern village believers belong on opposing sides of apparent ideological battlegrounds.

Consider the differences for what they tell us. In *Falling Man*, "God is the voice that says, 'I am not here.'" DeLillo's characters fear existence might be nothing more "than our own dank fluids." *Gilead* counters with a God-filled universe full of theological reference. The Reverend Ames ponders what he will look like in heaven and writes to more than his six-year-old son. Like John Calvin in the sixteenth century, Ames believes "each of us is an actor on a stage and God is the audience."

Place is a variable that tells us who we are, and it, too, functions through extremes in the settings of the two novels. DeLillo's New Yorkers are anonymous wanderers. Robinson's villagers live grounded and knowing everyone's business. Location in New York City means apartments with borrowed art on the walls. When DeLillo's characters move, they hold on to almost nothing. In Gilead, place is the land and houses known by the names of their owners and the furniture in them. Robinson's descriptions are elegiac, but if her touchstones are poignant, neither the land nor the houses on it provide as they once did. Many of the named owners have left the village.

Communal trouble defines both places, but the nature of the troubled is not an agreed-upon condition in these novels. Faces are mirrored falsehoods in DeLillo. "There is nothing more astonishing than a human face" in Robinson. Physicality defines character in DeLillo. Not so in Robinson, where "when someone dies the body is just an old suit of clothes the spirit doesn't want anymore." Adultery is a shallow interlude in *Falling Man*. Mere seduction rips a family apart in *Gilead*. Thought in *Falling Man* is "the noise the brain makes." Contemplation is the mark of grace in *Gilead*.

These differences belong to national divisions. The cosmopolitanism of DeLillo's coastal setting and the traditional values of Robinson's heartland have created fault lines that set twenty-first-century Americans against each other, but it is a consuming similarity that has made their debates so acrimonious.

Falling Man and *Gilead* jointly bespeak our times because they are consumed by the same compulsive sense of loss, and it is a sense of loss that extends to every level—personal, communal, and national. Both novels see an America as much less than it has been. Something intrinsic but hard to describe has been lost or at least seriously damaged. DeLillo and Robinson depict a nation adrift from its moorings and in need of anchoring, but like political debate in the nation, they disagree over the way to anchor and hence over the means of recovery.

What are we to make of this deeply felt inchoate sense of loss as an assumption about American life today? It is everywhere in these novels and all the more intriguing when DeLillo and Robinson make the same claim with such certainty from opposite temperamental and ideological directions.

Falling Man

More than any other writer of our time, Don DeLillo writes of isolated figures on the edge of catastrophe. *White Noise* (1985), *Mao II* (1991), and *Underworld* (1997) prove the point, but they are topped by *Falling Man* in 2007. This fourteenth novel, based as it is on a real event, feeds DeLillo's habitual need to warn the world against itself. *Falling Man* turns admonition into omen. It dares to tell both sides, attacker and victim, in the surprise attack on the World Trade Center.

In *Harper's Magazine*, just two months after the attack on September 11, 2001, DeLillo already has decided the crucial points that will shape *Falling Man* six years later. "The catastrophic event," he writes there, "changes the way we think and act"; "the world narrative belongs to terrorists." Consequently, anyone who wishes to respond must come up with "a new counter-narrative."

But how is this response to be made when "there is no logic in apocalypse," when "the event itself has no purchase on the mercies of analogy or simile"? In a fantastic wild assault by a very small group of men, two of the tallest buildings in the world, rising 110 stories above the ground—buildings that are not just "emblems" of modernity but "justifications" of it—collapse into rubble in less than an hour and a half with almost three thousand innocent people dead and buried inside.

This new species of devastation spawns an image that further complicates the facts, and DeLillo uses the same *Harper's* article to prove that it is indeed an image that controls thought. "Before politics, before history and religion there is the primal terror," he writes. "People falling from the towers hand in hand." Even with this image in place, the novelist seems to have given himself an impossible task. "The writer," he insists, "tries to give memory, tenderness, and meaning to all that howling space."

But what if, as T. S. Eliot claims in "The Dry Salvages," "there is no end of it, the voiceless wailing"? What if the noise in all of that howling space drowns meaningful perception in horror? DeLillo's answer, already this early in his thinking, controls what *Falling Man* will become. The *Harper's* article insists that we "name the future, not in our normally hopeful way but guided by dread."

Dread, by definition, feeds off the apprehension and then the comprehension of loss. It has many facets, and DeLillo's title uses the image of falling to convey five different levels of it. The novelist then uses these levels to reach for a sixth level of implication, his boldest stroke in search of counter-narrative. At this sixth level, *Falling Man* couples the terrorist attacker, defined by "medieval expedience," to his victim, defined by postmodern angst. DeLillo says there must be a bridge of explanation across the chasm.

A novel "guided by dread" logically isolates its characters in their perception of vulnerability. The word "dread" functions as either noun or verb, the objective fact as well as the active feeling, and both forms raise the same question. Will *the thing* feared get *me,* or will it get *someone else?* The descending levels of *Falling Man* carry these fears to nightmare depths, and the visceral image of falling controls them.

The term "Falling Man" refers *first* to the photograph of a doomed man plunging out of the burning North Tower; *second,* to a performance artist who reinvokes the image of "jumpers" from the towers when he leaps in a harness that catches him just before impact; *third,* and inevitably, to "The Fall of Man"; *fourth,* to the mental plunge of Alzheimer's patients who lose their hold on themselves and mirror "the timeless drift in the long spiral down" of those in the burning towers; *fifth,* to *failing man* in the protagonist's failure to meet his adult responsibilities; and *sixth,* to the discovery of a chilling similarity between the killing terrorist and the suffering victim, a lowest common denominator that helps to explain both.

The interwoven realizations of these levels, their collective implications, reinforce each other, and each requires a meaningful spectator. Transfixed and horrified, someone must always "see the fall" for it to happen. To plunge in either physical terror or mental collapse takes away the meaning of the self. Recourse lies in the compassion of a knowing observer. Humanity depends on the fact and feeling of a survivor who apprehends and then comprehends with the integrity of a sincere witness.

Keith Neudecker's estranged wife, Lilanne Glenn, is DeLillo's symbolic onlooker across his fields of dread. Obsessed by 9/11 and shocked anew by jumps of the performance artist, she still manages to give of herself to others around her. Her task as a freelance editor has been to decipher an impenetrable manuscript for a publishing house, one of DeLillo's many indicators of a hopelessly confused world. But she also volunteers therapy sessions for Alzheimer's patients and copes as best she can with the near autism of a husband who "could not find himself in the things he saw and heard."

An accurate if bewildered witness, Lilanne suffers from paranoia after the attack. She begins to worry that taxicabs may deliberately run her down, but she rises above these feelings and handles the worst of what she sees with a level of reflection that carries beyond fear. DeLillo sticks to the isolation of his characters. Lilanne is his exception. She connects. We last see her "ready to be alone in reliable calm, she and the kid, the way they were before the planes appeared that day, silver crossing blue."

The last phrase conveys the struggle in what Lilanne has accomplished. She, like so many on that day, never sees the planes coming. No matter. "Silver crossing blue" now belongs to the figment of every New Yorker's imagination, the next surprise attack on the way. Lilanne slowly overcomes her fear by searching for her former self ("the way they were before"). The feeling of "lonely" slowly becomes "alone in reliable calm," in the victory that a healthy working solitude can bring.

What has allowed this recovery to take place? Lilanne's realization of herself against what others endure eases her dread. She is the one who asks questions in search of answers. By persevering, she becomes the best DeLillo can hope for through "identity and memory and human heat." These elements form the basis of humanity. They supply the empathy and consideration that mark the best in the living as they watch the dying jump by the hundreds from the flames of the burning towers.

DeLillo easily ties the jumpers to the image of "falling man," a phrase that works because it is not his own. Another writer, Tom Junod, used the term in a memorial article for *Esquire* magazine on the second anniversary of 9/11, four years before the publication of *Falling Man*. Junod applied it to a spontaneous photograph taken by journalist Richard Drew of a victim plunging from the tower. In Junod's description of the photograph, the flicker of Drew's lens gives grace and form to death:

> He departs from this earth like an arrow. Although he has not chosen his fate, he appears to have in his last instants of life, embraced it. If he were not falling, he might very well be flying.

He appears relaxed, hurtling through the air.
He appears comfortable in the grip of unimagi-
nable motion. He does not appear intimidated
by gravity's divine suction or what awaits him.
His arms are by his side, only slightly outrig-
gered. His left leg is bent at the knee, almost
casually. . . . [He] is perfectly vertical, and so is
in accord with the lines of the buildings behind
him. He splits them, bisects them: Everything
to the left of him in the picture is in the North
Tower; everything to the right, the South. . . .
There is something almost rebellious in the
man's posture, as though once faced with the
inevitability of death, he decided to get on with
it; as though he were a missile, a spear, bent on
attaining his own end.

The passage ties form to wish fulfillment. Held upside
down or sideways, the image does indeed present a man
flying, even though he is falling. Junod's many qualifiers—
"appear," "might," "almost," and "as though"—are therefore crucial. The photograph tells a truth in the staggered
moment and a lie in kinetic time.

Frozen in the image, "falling man" exudes poise, but
in the next flicker of the lens, not shown in Junod's article, he is one more tormented victim thrashing and
flailing like all the other jumpers struggling for life
while falling at 150 miles per hour. The controlled act of
will—"attaining his own end"—belongs to the photo-

graph. In life, the falls from the towers accelerated at an impossible thirty-two feet per second squared and consumed ten full seconds before "the booming, rattling explosions the jumpers made upon impact."

The fastidious compulsions of modern existence confine end of life to hospices, care centers, hospitals, and funeral homes. Many Americans have never seen death, much less violent death. The jumpers from the twin towers gave everyone there a view of it. The ability to watch people fall from the heights mesmerized viewers as much as the attack. Bodies plunging are what people, including DeLillo, remember most.

The photograph of "falling man" succeeds because it changes dying for the living. It gives back a measure of control to an impossible event. It allows the helpless victim, and by extension all victims, a dignity in death. It does something else as well. The formal bearing of "falling man" domesticates dread. The image of loss so perfectly alone is a blessing. It restores individual worth to a revolting massacre of thousands of innocent lives that had no time to prepare for their terrible end.

How, then, does an artificial fall change the situation? What are DeLillo's purposes in giving us an ersatz falling man? The calculated falls of the performance artist oscillate between memorial and voyeuristic display. The actor dropping headfirst in his harness remembers the jumpers, and he doesn't want anyone on the ground to forget them. The formalities of air and ground are rehearsed, but in a debased way. Some things cannot be approached. In Junod's *Esquire* article, he reports "those tumbling through the air remained, by all accounts, eerily silent; those on the ground screamed."

Perhaps one cannot continue to scream falling from so high, so alone, and faster and faster, but if so, the screams from the ground share humanity about to be lost. They tally with the held hands of the jumpers in a spontaneity that has no place on the stage of the performance artist. When the victim has no hope, when there is nothing to be done, the only answer is a mutual grasp, hands held together in recognition of a fate to be met now and recognized in collective agony below.

There is a world of difference between this moment and a simulated moment. One had to watch if one was there. But what of the character in *Falling Man* who says in disappointment, "I didn't see them holding hands. I wanted to see that." Coming after, the would-be "seer" belongs to the time frame of the performance artist. Memory and entertainment cross in morbid confirmation of what happened. Curiosity wants its horror vicariously. It craves the wonder in disaster from the sanitized distance of television.

The actor secure in his harness performs "the puppetry of human desperation," and DeLillo alludes to the audiences who are "outraged at the spectacle" in a gesture that reaches obliquely back to himself. The novelist, too, is a performance artist, a voyeur using 9/11, as have so many others in the wake of the event.

Using the tragedy of the towers—an untouchable event—yields a pejorative response hard to avoid. The performance artist awakens disgust in some, perchance even in himself, and the debates about him in *Falling Man* suggest there is no proper stance to 9/11 beyond the literal one. Keith Neudecker, in his effort to get past check lines while returning to his own home near the World Trade Center, supplies it. Basically mute and without further explanation, he says over and over again, "I'm standing here." The event defies later possession. Everything pales against the original presence.

Some who insist on an explanation of what happened turn to DeLillo's third level of dread, "The Fall of Man," a doctrine in which all of humanity is lost. Several characters in the novel want to know where is God when the towers fall. "If God let this happen, with the planes," asks one, "then did God make me cut my finger when I was slicing bread this morning?" The problem exists beyond scale. "We sit and listen and God tells us or doesn't," responds another. But that answer explains little. "What about the people God saved?" asks a believer. "Are they better people than the ones who died?"

The answer not given to this last question is clear in theological doctrine, not that DeLillo gives it. In "The Fall of Man" no one deserves to be saved because all are sinful. Brutally, DeLillo places all these questions in the faltering minds of his Alzheimer's patients, a clear indication that God is no part of his own answer. On the other hand, Alzheimer's disease, his fourth level of dread with its technical name of "retrogenesis" (literally a falling out of creation), *is* one of DeLillo's answers.

In a novel about an act of terror, the ultimate terror is about losing one's sense of humanity as the terrorists have done. DeLillo's afflicted patients have "an elemental fear out of deepest childhood" that we all share. They don't know where they are or who they are. The world is "receding" from them; they are "not lost so much as falling." Lost words they once knew correspond to Keith Neudecker's trauma. When wounded and still in the shock of survival, he "wonders what has happened to the meaning of things, to tree, street, stone, wind, simple words lost in the falling ash."

We all have to worry about losing our minds if we live long enough, and it haunts DeLillo's heroine Lilanne, the thinking person in the novel. She has lost her father to the disease, and he may have passed it to her genetically. She looks for "the breathless moment when things fall away, streets, names, all sense of direction and location." These terms are the very ones that describe the collapse of the towers.

DeLillo plays on this lurking form of dread, giving it plenty of space in *Falling Man*. He spares no one the prospect of the ultimate horror of an existence without meaning: "the lapse into eventual protein stupor." Along the way he recounts a special way of being alone: "I'm alone," claims one "receding" patient, "because that's who I am." Here, more than anywhere else in the novel, DeLillo gives negative truth its day and its coming long night, "mapped in slow and certain decline."

Other forms of decline easily attach to this one: "There's an empty space where America used to be," "the decline and fall of literate exchange," "you understand that it's all about loss," "most lives make no sense," "it seemed to her that they were falling out of the world." Falling man falls everywhere writ small and large: "a thousand heaving dreams, the trapped man, the fixed limbs, the dream of paralysis, the gasping man, the dream of asphyxiation, the dream of helplessness."

Keith Neudecker, the survivor, epitomizes this phenomenon. He is *falling man* as *failing man,* but he is not alone. The masterstroke of the novel comes in DeLillo's ability to tie this fifth level to a deeper sixth level of dread. The novelist gives us unsettling descriptions of withdrawal from all human affection on the part not only of Neudecker but also of the character Hammad, one of the terrorists on the attacking airplane.

Thus it is that *Falling Man* closes with Hammad and Neudecker merging in midsentence: the first man's reactions on the airplane become the second man's reactions inside the tower without missing a grammatical beat. In this, the eeriest of many parallels in the novel, the cameo appearance of Hammad mirrors the process of dehumanization that we follow more elaborately in Neudecker.

The terrorist learns to control his life in death by turning the lives of all others into an illusion. He makes all previous connections "fade into dust." He learns to accept "there are no others." For Hammad, this reductive capacity means "those who will die have no claim to their lives outside the useful fact of their dying."

Neudecker's distinct but comparable alienation makes use of the same reductive tendencies, and they allow him to ignore the responsibilities of his own making. Nearing forty years of age, long into marriage and paternity, he stops to ask himself, "How is it possible that he was about to become . . . husband and father, finally, occupying a room in three dimensions in the manner of his parents?"

"Self-sequestered," Neudecker hides in "a dimension of literal distance between himself and others." He is "a model" for his male friends "but sheer hell on women," another sure sign of arrested adolescence. He alone is responsible for the "extended grimness called their marriage," followed by their eighteen months of separation, but he hurries back to Lilanne for shelter and care from the collapsing towers, after which, in idleness, he spends his days correcting the spelling of his name on the mail he never opens. He is always somewhere else, "empty, neutral" with those closest to him.

The parallel to Hammad the terrorist continues in Neudecker's ever-deepening alienation. Before 9/11, he is happiest playing cards with his buddies, two of whom die in the twin towers, with a third critically injured. DeLillo uses the excuse of these traumas to turn his character into a "robotic" card dealer in Las Vegas casinos. There he lives contented, carefully away from family and any connection with the nameless people around him.

Playing in binges, all day and night, Neudecker prefers the casino in the morning when it is "mostly empty of human pulse" and "stank of abandonment." He welcomes the arranged "narrowness of need or wish." He accurately and comfortably sees himself as "a self-operating mechanism, like a humanoid robot that understands two hundred voice commands, far-seeing, touch-sensitive, but totally, rigidly controllable." The same description applies quite readily and directly to Hammad the terrorist, who has programmed himself to be an automaton on his way into the twin towers.

What can possibly be said for Keith Neudecker's choices? Yes, the trauma of the towers has injured him psychologically, but it also seems to have confirmed his inner nature. DeLillo is clear about this. "He was never more himself than in these rooms with a dealer crying out a vacancy at table seventeen," Neudecker observes in confirmation of his choices. Like Hammad, he succeeds by "making a point of not getting interested" in anything or anyone who happens to be around him.

The greatest danger in terrorism and in life becomes this narrowness in temperament, a falling out of humanity. Neudecker shares with Hammad the desire to let others do the thinking. The internalized card player enjoys the fact "there was nothing outside the game but faded space." Putting everything else aside simplifies things. Space, it turns out, is one of Hammad's favorite words as well. "What they hold so precious we see as empty space," he concludes of Americans in limiting his view of them.

Both men, the terrorist and his victim, avoid a complicated view of value and limit their understandings to a mechanical mission. Unfortunately, the victim's mission is picayune in comparison. The postmodern world-weariness of Neudecker—defined by each "new deck" of cards—is trapped in self-imposed boredom. The card player refuses "the effort it takes to hear what is always there." At this sixth philosophical level, DeLillo seems bent on proving that "the world narrative" really does "belong to terrorists."

Hammad, the terrorist, restricts his own vision but with more devastating consequences. Because he is incomprehensible in the consumer culture that America has become, he easily reduces it to its trivialities when he argues "this entire life, this world of lawns to water and hardware stacked on endless shelves, was total, forever, an illusion." Neudecker, the compulsive card player in casinos, gives more than a little metaphysical credence to Hammad's claim of meaningless illusion.

The card player's philosophy of life is one of mundane evasion, and it conveys a typicality in him that defines many others in postmodern society. How many people do you know who handle their time alone and sense of worth through mastery of a game or activity, either by participating in it or simply watching it obsessively? Virtually all of American television is given over to trivial pursuits of one kind or another. Much of consumer culture seems to be about marking time in it.

Terrorist and victim, in their separate but linked constipation in thought, have decided their lives are worthless within the endless possibilities that life provides. Hammad, in the moment before his death, says, "All of life's lost time is over now." Neudecker at the card tables dismisses time in comparable ways. "There were no days or times except for the tournament schedule," he concludes.

Each man, the terrorist and his traumatized victim, welcomes incapacity, a tight restriction on the range in thought that is rigidly maintained. The counternarrative is therefore less "a counter" than "a parallel," one in which neither position has an appeal that can be deciphered.

Nothing can be said for the quality of the choices that either man makes except to notice in some dismay that their mutually reductive patterns eliminate the problem of being lonely while alone. Each man leaches away all possibility of relationship, much less of intimacy. The parallels meet only in poverty of thought. Neither character can find or accept worth in another human being.

DeLillo's counter-narrative therefore does not answer the terrorist so much as it tries to explain that mentality in terms that a postmodern victim might understand. But is that enough? Do we have a counter-narrative or merely the same narrative explained in different voice? Lost in loss, the terrorist and his postmodern victim have both forgotten that we know only as we learn to love. The counter-narrative that Keith Neudecker is meant to epitomize is of little worth to anyone interested in the value or even the inclinations of life.

Gilead

The house of the Reverend John Ames, in contrast, is full of love and value. It is also laced with regret. As John Ames's young wife says ever so gently to her dying husband, "Why'd you have to be so damned old?'" But the best of life is still now. Ames in his twenties lost a wife and baby daughter in childbirth and has lived alone for almost half a century until this mysterious young woman in her thirties, "a fine vital woman like she is," asks him to marry her and gives him the ideal son he thought he would never have. Even Ames has to admit all of this has been "something more than a miracle."

Gilead is thus another daydream of good aging. It is the quintessential elder novel. It celebrates not just independence in old age but rebirth, harmony, fulfillment, and perceived worth in the eyes of all who know the protagonist. "I live in a light better than any dream of mine," Ames declares. Although fatally ill, he retains the strength of a vital man who can say with conviction, "I'd rather drop dead doing for myself than add a day to my life by acting helpless." How many of us have said as much, but how many get to have the good death that Robinson promises her protagonist?

All this happiness aside, the novel works through a blasted early life of loneliness. Ames has found his first balance in hard-won solitude after terrible loss. His second balance depends on the knowledge of that loss and his ensuing gratitude for the family that would ordinarily belong to a much younger man.

Both periods in life are philosophically valuable, but the key to his life and thought remains the time of earlier isolation that he has overcome on his own. "My own dark time, as I call it," he says, "the time of my loneliness, was most of my life . . . and I can't make any real account of myself, without speaking of it." The ability developed in solitude defines the writer of the memoir.

That said, everyone in Robinson's story lives more or less alone without being lonely. The loving family is a silent one. We hardly ever hear the voice of Mrs. Ames, and we don't so much as learn her first name, Lila, until we hear it from a visitor two hundred pages into the novel. The six-year-old son who plays on his own, seemingly as quiet by nature as his parents, provides another muted mystery.

We never question the loving nature of this family. It runs, though, on a noiseless awareness explained in apprehension. Robinson's stylistic choices must take some responsibility here. A certain thinness in secondary characters may be the inevitable consequence of a monologue driven by other concerns.

The center of narrative awareness in *Gilead* is that Ames is dying as he holds desperately onto life. "Existence seems to me now," he writes, "the most remarkable thing that could ever be imagined." His goal in leaving a memoir for his son is to win a degree of permanence against loss and dissolution. To return for a moment to Shakespeare through the qualified affirmation in Sonnet 65, Ames hopes "that in black ink my love may still shine bright." "While you read this," the memoir claims to the loved son for whom it is intended, "I am imperishable, somehow more alive than I have ever been."

But how are we to take this assumption in plot terms? It comes as instruction to the boy of six who will read Ames's words only much later if at all, and Robinson has given us a novel in which no son ever agrees with the plan or advice of the father before him across three generations. Much of the novel recounts the conflicts between fathers and sons, most of whom have been ministers. *Gilead* posits a special loneliness through the assertion that each generation must fight its own battles its own way.

The seemingly static village world of Gilead is thereby as full of change as DeLillo's New York City. Nothing isolates in American life like the constant change in it. Ames assumes his grown son will have nothing to do with Gilead, "a shabby little town you will no doubt leave behind," and he wonders whether his wife will also leave the town he has given his life to when he is gone.

The crisis in what Ames writes out for his son comes here. His words are a quest for permanence against a future that will not allow it.

Rebellious sons are the sign of mutability. Ames writes as "the good son" in the knowledge of an older brother, Edward, who broke with their father only to have the father embrace the prodigal and turn against the traditional path and purpose that John Ames has followed in the name of the father. In the turnover of the generations, no generation appears capable of pleasing another.

Robinson adds tension to her story by bringing the most rebellious of sons back to Gilead. John Ames Boughton, "Jack," is the son of another minister in town, Ames's best friend, and, as the full name implies, Jack is John Ames's godson but no soul mate. Jack has been an unscrupulous seducer and troublemaker all his life. Soon he appears interested in Ames's young wife, and Ames naturally resents what might happen when he is gone, but this resentment, it turns out, is misplaced. Robinson uses it adroitly. She exploits it to indicate how the old always doubt the young, how jealousy can infect the most honest life, how the dying cannot help but envy the living.

The side plot of the troublemaker who actually causes no trouble seems extraneous until one remembers Robinson's purposes. The no longer dangerous "Jack" has been beaten down by life. He reinforces a sadness that permeates the novel, and his presence humanizes John

Ames by giving him a fault or two. The novelist slips in a touching truth: "there is guilt enough in the best life," and Ames is made to realize it in himself. "There's a lot under the surface of life," he writes, "everyone knows that. A lot of malice and dread and guilt, and so much loneliness, where you wouldn't really expect to find it."

The understanding that loneliness is found even where one wouldn't expect it is a crucial observation with universal application. Loneliness is the feeling that people are reluctant to discuss however intensely it is felt. The controlling theme of Robinson's book belongs to an inherent loneliness through loss hidden but known. Known, in this sense of the word, means more than recognition of the plight. The answer to loss is the soul's knowledge of itself, pared down and separated, in a way that it must learn to accept.

Here, as well, is the underlying philosophical divide from *Falling Man*. Keith Neudecker and Hammad, in DeLillo's accounts, are never ready to face the self on its own terms. They need externalities to compensate for a hollowness within. John Ames in *Gilead* takes on the assignment of self-knowledge through the solitude that has made him more than his loneliness. "I don't know why solitude would be a balm for loneliness," he humbly reports, "but that is how it always was for me."

Solitude welcomed encourages a mental adventure of worthy proportions, a life story told with as much truth as the speaker can bear. In trying to tell his life from beginning to end, Ames reaches beyond the self through the self that is disappearing. "A prevenient courage" keeps him on track. It says, "Precious things have been put into our hands, and to do nothing to honor them is to do great harm."

By explaining what is precious in the life that has been led, Ames hopes to convey the quality of what existence can be in his son. Two memories of happiness out of despair convey the tactile nature of life's commitments when one person reaches for another in the resilience of need against the resignation of loss.

In the first memory, Ames is a small child, like his own son, when a village church has burned, and the congregation has tried to save what cannot be saved in the arrival of a second sudden disaster, pouring rain:

> I lay under the wagon with the other little children, watching them pull down the ruins of that Baptist church, and my father brought me a piece of biscuit for my lunch, and I crawled out and knelt with him there, in the rain. I remember it as if he broke the bread and put a bit of it in my mouth, though I know he didn't. His hands and his face were black with ash—he looked charred, like one of the old martyrs—and he knelt there in the rain and brought a piece of biscuit out of his shirt, and he did break it, that's true, and gave half to me and ate the other half himself.

As one generation gives to another out of "the bread of affliction," so that next generation offers what is possible to a new one in John Ames to his son: "I leave to you but the ruins of old courage and the lore of old gallantry and hope."

The passage sings through imagination used but checked. Memory has improved on the earlier reality. Nevertheless, the accuracy of that reality is what must be passed down the line for it to have meaning. The real bread was "given" and only imagined to be more symbolically and religiously "put in the mouth." The earlier father and son, against later differences, share a spontaneous communion amidst loss and devastation. Their connection, not the disaster, gives meaning to the child, and Ames implicitly asks his own small son to experience a similar recognition against his own disaster through the integrity of the words offered to him.

The second memory is unbearably fresh. It comes at the end, and it anticipates the death of the writer before it happens:

> Your mother seems to want every supper to be my favorite supper. There is often meat loaf, and always dessert. She puts candles on the table, since dark is coming early now. I suspect she has brought them from the church, and that's all right. Often she wears her blue dress. You have outgrown your red shirt. Old Boughton's family have gathered, except the one his

> heart yearns for. They pay their respects and
> invite us for dinner, but these days we three
> love to be at home. You come in reeking of eve-
> ning air, with your eyes bright and your cheeks
> and fingers pink and cold, too beautiful in the
> candlelight for my old eyes. The cold has si-
> lenced all the insects. The dark seems to make
> us speak softly, like gentle conspirators.

"These days" are the last days. Winter approaches, and
the writer will not see it, much less survive it. The in-
sects, symbols of passing, have already been "silenced"
by the cold of descending death.

Lila Ames does everything she can to make these "last
suppers" the best of life for her husband, even as he lives
the best of life. The candles are a votive offering to what
the three have been together, and yet the unknowing
child has already outgrown the favorite garment that
his father likes to see him wear; he is the coming of
change that will not remember as it casts present things
aside.

This wonderfully alive "pink" child is also too precious or "beautiful" for the dying father to look upon
except through a veil of tears. He is losing his son as
surely as "Old Boughton" has lost his. The conspiracy is
of death unspoken by the two parents. Still, the writer
can hope that his son will remember something of him
through meals so often repeated and continuing when
his father is no longer at the table.

We know ourselves through the stories that we truthfully tell about ourselves, separating out the distortions that we sometimes add and that can cause us to lose ourselves. Ames has done that much and more. He has given meaning to himself and others through the love that he so accurately tells. This love in connection is always possible but never probable. Writing it out against the loss that will take it away lets it happen again. Love, like the writing, finds its proof in the effort it always requires.

The perspective that such an effort requires differentiates John Ames from others. If you have taken the measure of your life and accomplished what it was possible for you to accomplish against a sea of loss, you have done all that can be asked of you by anyone, including yourself. There are no perfect lives, but there is the self-knowledge of a life that has understood itself in recognition with others. The integrity that goes into that communication is even more. It is the gain conceived against the loss known.

IO

WALT WHITMAN FINDS
THE COURAGE TO BE

Courage is the fourth of the cardinal virtues after justice, wisdom, and moderation. Most accounts place it last, and its icon is the lion, not the human figure used to depict the first three virtues. Courage is different. Although it requires at least as much effort as the other virtues, it draws peculiarly on ideas of risk. Unlike the others, courage means taking a personal chance in a hazardous undertaking. The figure of the lion as symbol suggests danger and raw physicality as well as bravery.

Because it is also situational, courage is difficult to characterize in the abstract, and it is easily lost in an uncertain, unexpected, strange, or hopeless occasion. So powerful is the element of context in courage that it can rearrange the pantheon of the virtues. The ancients lived in a world full of sudden challenges, and they knew that without courage none of the other virtues mattered in a crisis.

What will one risk in a crisis? Paul Tillich in *The Courage to Be* takes up the problem in just this way. "Courage," he writes, "always includes a risk," and the nature of it is essentially twofold. We either lose ourselves "becoming a thing within the whole of things," or we lose the "world in an empty self-relatedness." If you have the courage to act but fail, you are crushed by the whole of things; if you lack that courage when needed, you fall into a void of communal and self disregard.

Either way, the enemy is the same; we succumb to a form of "nonbeing." Courage answers this anxiety by demanding the understanding and the need for action as the choice and duty and meaning of life. Tillich says to live is to push against the uncertainties that press against us. "The courage to take the anxiety of meaninglessness upon oneself is the boundary line up to which the courage to be can go."

To understand the risk in pushing against boundary lines, physical or mental, we need a figure who challenges them with unique daring. In 1855 he is "Walt Whitman, a kosmos," but also and more forlornly, "solitary me." The doubled autobiographical figure in "Song of Myself" expands infinitely and contracts terribly. The distance between is the courage of the writer putting himself on the page "undisguised and naked" and declaring all "creeds and schools in abeyance."

Whitman opens "Song of Myself," this way: "I, now thirty-seven years old in perfect health begin, / Hoping to cease not till death." The connection of physicality, age, and health to the idea of death in a first introductory poem prepares us for a time when health may not be perfect, when age might interfere, when writing will be more difficult, when death might be more terrifying.

Two decades later and failing, Whitman faces these issues directly, personally, and painfully in *Specimen Days,* the forgotten prose masterpiece of a great poet. The concerns expressed in this late collection challenge the earlier poet and give us another reason for turning to the life rendered in it. The older Whitman, perhaps more than any other major figure in our literature, sees the lords of life for what they are: *failure, betrayal, change, defeat, fear, difference, age,* and *loss.*

Failure, betrayal, and *defeat* were Whitman's perpetual lot under the fastidious critical gaze of the nineteenth century. *Change* and *difference* defined Whitman's secret life in postbellum New York. *Fear, age,* and *loss* arrive in the collapse of the body and in the death of important family members all around him. Whitman writes *Specimen Days* in acute recognition that the end is near. Time is running out. As he quietly notes in his introduction, "If I do it at all, I must delay no longer."

In many ways this late, seemingly haphazard book is barely done. When the loosely strewn pages of *Specimen Days* finally appear in 1882, "incongruous and full of skips and jumps," "all bundled up and tied by a big string," they are ignored, and they remain undervalued. Reading Whitman's memoir requires effort. It also rewards effort. *Specimen Days* is the most accomplished monody on overcoming the fear of death through the idea of death that we have in American literature.

Whitman first comes to grips with the phenomenon like no other major writer of his day by tending to thousands of dying soldiers in the army hospitals of the Civil War. In an early section of *Specimen Days* entitled "The Real War Will Never Get in the Books," he summarizes what he has learned as a wound-dresser in words that explain the impulses and direction of the rest of the memoir: "So much of a race depends on how it faces death, how it stands personal anguish and sickness."

With the stoicism of the dying soldier as his figurative epigraph, Whitman offers his own brand of courage against a host of problems that rob him of that first original identity "in perfect health." *Specimen Days* comes to life against paralyzing strokes, familial tragedies, and derision over everything he has published.

There is much to overcome. Influential critics like Thomas Carlyle, William Dean Howells, and William James ridicule the poet as a primitive writer stuck in simplicity, vulgarity, ignorance, and empty optimism. These views prevail through Whitman's lifetime, and he knows they will continue to discourage attention after he is gone.

Carlyle, whose words bother Whitman the most, jokes about "the fellow who thinks he must be a big man because he lives in a big country." "It is as though the town-bull had learned to hold a pen." The poetry is literally excrement. Whitman resembles "a buffalo, useful in fertilizing the soil, but mistaken in supposing that his contributions of that sort are matters which the world desires to contemplate closely."

What kind of courage does it take to stand up to entrenched decorum, especially the kind that is as cruel and sophisticated as it is unfair? Whitman writes out the "knot of contrariety" as well as anyone. Nothing is simplistic. A sophisticated struggle with meaning dominates poems like "Crossing Brooklyn Ferry," "Out of the Cradle Endlessly Rocking," "As I Ebb'd with the Ocean of Life," and "When Lilacs Last in the Dooryard Bloom'd."

Whitman knows better than to answer his critics in poetry. *Specimen Days* is the better vehicle. It appears as a quiet but penetrating prose answer to those who have so willfully misunderstood him. More usefully for today's reader, it copes with the accelerating accumulation of losses, humiliations, and personal difficulties all around him with a poise and penetration that anyone facing similar difficulties would do well to imitate.

So different from the common herds of people whom he admires, Whitman is especially thoughtful on the theme and on the courage needed to overcome isolation.

He is committed to the connections that are still possible to him in *Specimen Days,* and reconfigures the major philosophical query of his time to prove that commitment in response to his critical nemesis. In the section entitled "Carlyle from American Points of View," we find the following comment in interrogatory form:

> What is the fusing explanation and tie—what the relation between the (radical, democratic) Me, the human identity of understanding, emotions, spirit, etc., on the one side, of and with the (conservative) Not Me, the whole of the material objective universe and laws, with what is behind them in time and space, on the other side?

The effort in Romanticism to trust an ephemeral subjectivity forces its proponents to ask questions like this one; but deeper into the question is an assertion when Whitman declares it "the most profound theme that can occupy the mind of man." The price of primacy on the self is lonely dissolution. When will the "Me" pass into the "Not Me," and what will it mean? As a later poet, Philip Larkin, writes in *Aubade:*

> Most things may never happen: this one will,
> And realisation of it rages out
> In furnace-fear

Whitman's fear of nonbeing is acute in his discussions of Carlyle. The Scottish intellectual has given the world an original formulation of the "Me" and the "Not Me," and since he is a philosophical skeptic, Whitman pauses over "the thought Of Carlyle dying" to wonder what "the mysteries of death and genius" could have meant to such a thinker in that lonely penultimate moment.

Predictably, Whitman concentrates on the physicality of Carlyle's body, now separate from thought. His choice of imagery may represent a form of payback for the animal imagery in Carlyle's satire of him, but much more is at stake. "And now that he has gone hence," Whitman asks, "can it be that Thomas Carlyle, soon to chemically dissolve in ashes and by winds, remains an identity still?"

Ralph Waldo Emerson has already solved this anxiety for himself by dividing the same formula in an exacting way. In *Nature* from 1836, the "Me" is composed entirely of Soul or Spirit; the "Not Me," "all that is separate from us," comprises everything else, including, for Emerson, "my own body." By separating the body from the essential self, Emerson leaves himself a logical path to immortality.

This choice is not open to the poet of the body. If physicality is ignored by Emerson (and regretted by Henry Thoreau), Whitman cannot escape the body or its theoretical significance. As the very first poem in *Leaves of Grass* announces, "Of physiology from top to toe I sing." All of Whitman's integrity as a writer joins the body to the soul, and the connection means that he faces a graver epistemological predicament.

The poet of "Song of Myself" can "dote on myself, there is that lot of me and all so luscious," and he can add in "Crossing Brooklyn Ferry" "That I was, I knew was of my body." Heightened physicality is fundamental to the writer's identity and knowledge of self, but will dissolution of the body take the soul with it? Recall the festering corpse of Carlyle! Whitman leaves it on the examination table, where, after a very short period of time, it must "chemically dissolve" into nothing.

Time passing naturally compounds the problem of the body, and the place to see it is in the pages of *Specimen Days*. The poet of 1855 boasts, "If I worship one thing more than another it shall be the spread of my own body." In 1882, he must deal with the body's retreat and betrayal. The memoir is the work of an author suddenly old. Whitman suffers two strokes in his early fifties, starting in 1873, and he writes in fear of a much worse and perhaps final attack at any moment.

Contraction in the worshipped body raises the issue of nonbeing in the starkest terms. So central is decline to the writer of *Specimen Days* that he thinks of calling his book *Notes of a Half-Paralytic*. Nor is lost health the only problem in the 1870s. The mother he values above any other person and two brothers die. Quarrels, insanity, alcoholism, and prostitution rend a dysfunctional family. Whitman loses his government position, his only source of income. Literary luminaries reject or ignore his poetry, printers refuse to publish *Leaves of Grass* as an obscene work, friendships atrophy, and companions disappear.

Specimen Days is the transcending response to all these issues, and as such, it is a sourcebook for anyone in trouble. Given every reason to despair, Whitman refuses to give in to it, and in refusing, he writes out an antidote for himself and anyone who will listen. A life that has seen more distress and loneliness than most lives continues to hold itself erect in curiosity and exploration.

A rough, even loose compilation by the author's own admission, *Specimen Days* is still a life ordered, and it responds to the attritions and the inevitable problems of old age. Whitman has written a manual for coping with desolation. His book transforms loneliness into equanimity, and his tools for getting there form a balance. The tools are the healing possibility in solitude up against a counter-insistence that self-definition can only come through close observation and appreciation of the world around him.

Loneliness certainly appears in these pages. Right after his troubled comments on Carlyle, Whitman describes a pair of kingfishers. They are "full of free fun and motion," "the two together flying and whirling around." When the birds suddenly depart, Whitman just as quickly assumes all "frolics are deferred," and his conclusion is a non sequitur, except for what we know of the writer's isolation.

The last lines of the passage about the kingfishers carry the claim that the lines themselves are "curiously appropriate in more ways than one," but they remain unnamed. They come, in fact, from a poem by Coleridge with the arresting title "Work Without Hope":

> And I, the while, the sole unbusy thing,
> Nor honey make, nor pair, nor build, nor sing.

Hidden in these words are untold dimensions of loss, idleness, regret, loneliness, sadness, and time flown.

An answering solitude responds. Whitman invokes it in every scene of nature. In "The Great Unrest of Which We Are Part," he sits "in solitude and half-shade by the creek," musing on "the two impetuses of man and the universe." Here again is the vexed problem of the "Me" and the "Not Me." Nature signifies "change, in all its visible, and still more its invisible processes." Unfortunately, in changing, nature also signifies that time is running out for the observer. Can the "Me" answer? "What is humanity in its faith, love, heroism, poetry, even morals," Whitman answers, "but *emotion?*"

The key to psychological power in *Specimen Days* resides in Whitman's singular use of the word "emotion." Four late sections—"A Discovery of Old Age," "At Present Writing—Personal," "After Trying a Certain Book," and "Nature and Democracy"—give Whitman's understanding of the term. Taken together, they suggest how control of feeling encourages a hard-won happiness in the face of distress.

The poet who once celebrated feeling in "Spontaneous Me" now wishes to stay on top of feeling with more calculated purposes in mind. "Perhaps the best is always cumulative," he has learned. Here, in "A Discovery of Old Age," he notes "I discover the best hardly ever at first . . . stealthily opening to me, perhaps after years of unwitting familiarity, unappreciation, usage." This gradual approach to "the best" in experience, first discussed in "Seeing Niagara," depends on a new kind of perseverance. The later Whitman wants "some lucky five minutes of a man's life" for "remembrance always afterward."

Greater reliance on memory empowers one whose task has been clear throughout *Specimen Days*. "Seated here in solitude," Whitman explains in "Thoughts under an Oak," "I have been musing over my life—connecting events, dates, as links of a chain, neither sadly nor cheerily, but somehow . . . in an unusually matter-of-fact spirit." Retrospection soothes the owner of a spent life by recovering it.

The deepest tension in *Specimen Days* comes here in "Thoughts under an Oak." The writer contrasts his faltering life to the need for continuing adventure of the self-realized man, and there is much to praise in the effort. Whitman shows his awareness of both the divide and his response to it in "At Present Writing—Personal." "I easily tire," he writes, "am very clumsy, cannot walk far; but my spirits are first-rate."

Why, given such disability and personal tragedy, are Whitman's spirits still first-rate? The ailing writer unveils a second source of equanimity that seasons memory and counters loneliness. The world is a wonderful curiosity only if you maintain curiosity about it and bother to observe what is around you. "I keep up my activity and interest in life, people, progress, and the questions of the day."

Whitman's philosophical perspective helps here. Putting the "democratic" on the side of the "Me" in "the most profound theme that can occupy the mind of man" encourages Whitman, however limited he is in physical movement, to use everything around him. He is just as happy and important to us when watching mundane behavior in the waiting room of the Camden Ferry as he is bathing ecstatically in Nature.

Life must open to wherever the subjective and the objective meet. That way, it will find interest and, in the process, make itself interesting. Whitman puts this point succinctly in "After Trying a Certain Book." His mission can no longer be the melodrama of "wildness and frantic escapades," if it ever was. He writes now "to justify the soul's frequent joy in what cannot be defined."

Joy comes to the observer who watches the commonality all around without asking too much of it. The tiniest event often amuses Whitman, as we saw in appreciation of the momentary flight of the kingfishers. The "Me" in the older Whitman fuses with the "Not Me" not to explain itself, but to take the pleasure, the satisfaction, the awareness, and the grounding that the surprise in existence offers to anyone.

Claims of enjoyment match Whitman's underlying fear in *Specimen Days*. Over and over, the writer tells us how the ephemeral self must learn to accept and then use its moments. His stance resembles Walter de la Mare's moving lines from "Fare Well":

> Look thy last on all things lovely,
> Every Hour.

The very last lines of *Specimen Days* show again how this is to be done. Any attempt to rely on "sickly abstractions" will fail. Beauty, gratification, and meaning depend on appreciation of "the costless average, divine, original concrete." We must find what we need in the flow of ordinary events and situations.

The many scenes Whitman describes are delivered in a way that anyone can see and appreciate. They are meant to be shared. "What can be subtler and finer than this play of faces on such occasions in these responding crowds?" he asks as he watches throngs gather in "Departing of the Big Steamers." The comfort in these words depends upon an energy restored and then celebrated by watching the world at play and work. To accept an experience for what it can give and to remember it for what it meant to others is a reciprocity of realizations and a guard against the despair in loneliness.

The writer of *Specimen Days* flinches at nothing. "In diagnosing this disease called humanity," part of a section on "Edgar Poe's Significance," Whitman opts not for "the perfect character," but for "another shape of personality ... where the perfect character, the good, the heroic, although never attained, is never lost sight of, but through failures, sorrows, temporary downfalls, is returned to again and again."

The duty to restrict failures, sorrow, and downfalls is clear. It asks us to keep up "as long as mind, muscles, voice, obey the power we call volition." Perseverance, the form that courage requires in the long term, defines the personality that Whitman offers to his readers, and the reciprocities in this personality are everything to the success of *Specimen Days*. Whitman always has the knack of making a reader see him on the page, and he uses it here to make us observe the intrepid observer in every scene he describes.

Courage is more than a skill. It is the determination in emotional balance, and a form of self-creation. Consider the example of it given in "The Sky—Days and Nights—Happiness." Whitman dismisses Byron's assertion of personal misery. "Byron, just before his death, told a friend he had known but three happy hours during his whole existence." Whitman answers bluntly. We do not discover happiness or deserve it; we make it out of the tools given to us. "What is happiness, anyhow?" he asks. "Is this one of its hours or the like of it?—so impalpable—a mere breath, an evanescent tinge? I am not sure—so let me give myself the benefit of the doubt."

This benefit of the doubt, penned in 1876, must be understood against "the physical shatter and troubled spirit of me the last three years." Troubles test and wear us down. Whitman writes of his pain and fear, which are always there in what he calls "my own life-afternoon now arrived." The negatives in life, more than the positives, give integrity to Whitman's grasp of the passing moment.

The earlier poet sought "the brilliant sun." The prose writer knows that life quantified in the day is passing, and he tells us "as I grow old, the half-lights of evening are the more to me." Fear is a catalyst in his last pages. "So draw near their end these garrulous notes," writes the man often called too garrulous. Whitman wants us to glimpse the underlying anxieties that simmer through *Specimen Days*. Nonbeing when the "Me" enters the "Not Me" can come at any moment for the half-paralyzed writer.

Long gone is the poet of "Song of Myself" who boasts "Death . . . it is idle to try to alarm me." There he ends the poem by claiming "If you want me again look for me under your boot-soles." Old and sick in *Specimen Days,* he spends his last years raising money for a massive granite mausoleum that will sustain his name and hold him forever discrete from dissolution, away from the dirt of identity lost.

This architectural safeguard of identity has its structural parallel in *Specimen Days*. Whitman gives us a rare poem of his own in "A Quintette," and it registers the formula and balance of his pleasure in moments:

> At vacancy with Nature,
> Acceptive and at ease,
> Distilling the present hour,
> Whatever, wherever it is,
> And over the past, oblivion.

Yes, the writer is "acceptive and at ease" in keeping with his theory of observation, but the opening and closing words in the poem, "at vacancy" and "oblivion," present the fear in this poet, and the idea of "distillation" runs counter to his presumed stance. To distill means to refine against the spontaneity that the author so often claims for himself. There is masked trepidation about place in the reactive "whatever, wherever" of "the present hour."

Of course, spontaneity and calculation chase each other across the page in all of Whitman. More than any other literary figure of his time, he crafts an illusive persona that directs a reader through the loose improvisation of his writing. Confirmations of this persona, "the bonafide spirit and relations, from author to reader," dominate the last pages of *Specimen Days*. They are his final controlling device.

More than hints of a personal literary craft and presence begin to appear in "At Present Writing—Personal,"

"After Trying a Certain Book," and "Final Confessions—Literary Tests." Whitman uses his rejection of a book titled *The Theory of Poetry* to reveal how it is possible for him to hide while remaining in plain sight. "At its best," he responds, "poetic lore is like what may be heard of conversation in the dusk, from speakers far or hid.... What is not gathered is far more—perhaps the main thing," and yet the same passage admits that careful deliberations "make up the curious chessgame of a poem."

This suddenly demanding figure rips whole sections out of the books he reads. The ensuing "bunch of loose leaves," much like his own book, satisfies his "play of imagination" and "appetite of literature" while sustaining him "utterly out of reach of literary conventions." His challenge to those who dismiss his work comes in his request for a different kind of reader. "Has it never occurred to anyone how . . . any truly first-class production has little or nothing to do with the rules and calibres of ordinary critics?"

Meaning and therefore solace reside in the writer's connection to a willing reader over the communication of feeling. This is where "the bonafide spirit and relations, from author to reader" take hold. To secure you in *Specimen Days,* Whitman puts you time and again at the scene and looking at him. You are there, and each scene tells you what it is possible to be and feel when you see as he saw.

Whitman's real skill as a writer comes here. "Talent alone cannot make a writer," Emerson notes in

Representative Men. "There must be a man behind the book." He speaks of Goethe but might just as easily have been thinking of Whitman. We always see the man behind Whitman's words. It is the ultimate source of his craft. We know that *he* is *there.* All of Whitman's energy, integrity, and quest for permanence lives in this ability to present himself on the page in his own unique way. He knows it, and he makes you see it. The writer tells you he is there as long as you are there.

Whitman's greatest use of this strategy appears in "Crossing Brooklyn Ferry." He speaks to us in that poem from 1856 in a way that first acknowledges and then requires his own death. He tells us, "I am with you, you men and women of a generation, or ever so many generations hence, / Just as you feel when you look on the river and sky, so I felt." "What is the count of the scores or hundreds of years between us?" he asks, and the working poet's reply is the poem itself.

The final, hidden resource against loneliness and in favor of achieved solitude lies in shared moments of participation between this writer and the unknown but seized reader. Whitman's "days" can be our days. His days turn into "specimens" through the knowledge of our own. Literature can thus supersede the problems that divide us from each other and that keep us away from even ourselves. It is the provision across time of what we are to each other. What life once meant is what it can mean again.

The closing stance in *Specimen Days* honors this test of time in the same way that "Crossing Brooklyn Ferry" succeeds, but it takes more courage in the dying man to do it. In a sense, Whitman turns Paul Tillich's construct of courage on its head. He wills himself to become "a thing within the whole of things" without ever losing "self-relatedness." The writer removes himself into the death that he knows is coming soon. He deliberately turns himself over to a later time, to our time. We are "the disembodied human soul giving its verdict" on the page that is no longer his but ours.

Where does the courage to do this much come from? The lasting power in literature comes from the intimacy it gives to permanence. Whitman is the proven American master of this intimacy. He insists that it will carry him over his death into our lives. The loneliness and fear of the writer turn into the solitude that he shares with all future readers who stop to appreciate the effort he has given. But why should we do it? Why continue to read this often difficult book? Are there not many other ways to live our busy lives? The answers lie in the comfort available in connection, in another's understanding of us.

This power in literature is so great that it can reach across twenty-one centuries. The single best defense of the meaning that literature can supply comes before the birth of Christ and couched within a mundane legal argument. In 62 BCE Cicero rises in court in a humdrum and quite narrow if politically charged case to speak for an immigrant's right to remain in Rome. Suddenly, though, he is in full flight for us and all of time. Lost to history is whether or not Cicero wins his case, but that no longer matters in the most vital words of "Defense of the Poet Aulus Licinius Archias." The words have survived in part by accident but in part, no doubt, because so many have seen their value and willed them to survive.

What Cicero conveys to us touches every reader, to use a legal phrase, "from time out of memory." As with Whitman, a man whom we never knew, who lived in a world foreign to us, and whom we might not have liked or understood if we had known him, appears by our side. Here is what Cicero said in court and now says again, in a wonderfully succinct statement about what literature does to life:

> There is no other occupation upon earth that is so appropriate to every time and every age and every place. Reading stimulates the young and diverts the old, increases one's satisfaction when things are going well, and when they are going badly provides refuge and solace. It is a delight in the home; it can be fitted in with public life; throughout the night, on journeys, in the country, it is the companion that never lets me down.

The companion that never lets us down! Cicero suggests that literature begins as "a delight in the home," but for the knowing reader it *is* the home. It is wherever you happen to be, the domesticating scene of thought always available—not lost, forgotten, or taken away.

BIBLIOGRAPHY

PROLOGUE: THE LORDS OF LIFE

Primary Texts

Emerson, Ralph Waldo. "Experience." In *Essays: Second Series* [1844]. Vol. 3 of *The Collected Works of Ralph Waldo Emerson,* edited by Joseph Slater, Alfred R. Ferguson, and Jean Ferguson Carr, 25–49. Cambridge, MA: Belknap Press of Harvard University Press, 1983.

Background Reading

Archer, Margaret S. *Structure, Agency and the Internal Conversation.* New York: Cambridge University Press, 2003.

Barbour, John D. *The Value of Solitude: The Ethics and Spirituality of Aloneness in Autobiography.* Charlottesville: University of Virginia Press, 2004.

Cacioppo, John T., and William Patrick. *Loneliness: Human Nature and the Need for Social Connection*. New York: W. W. Norton, 2008.

Dumm, Thomas. *Loneliness as a Way of Life*. Cambridge, MA: Harvard University Press, 2008.

Flesch, William. *Comeuppance: Costly Signaling, Altruistic Punishment, and Other Biological Components of Fiction*. Cambridge, MA: Harvard University Press, 2007.

Klienenberg, Eric. *Going Solo: The Extraordinary Ride and Surprising Appeal of Living Alone*. New York: Penguin Press, 2012.

Koch, Philip. *Solitude: A Philosophical Encounter*. Chicago: Open Court, 1994.

Lewis, Kevin. *Loneliness: The Spiritual Meaning of American Solitude*. New York: I. B. Tauris, 2009.

Long, Christopher R., and James R. Averill. "Solitude: An Exploration of Benefits of Being Alone." *Journal for the Theory of Social Behavior* 33 (2003): 21–44.

Merton, Thomas. *The Silent Life*. New York: Farrar, Straus & Cudahy, 1957.

Mitchell, Charles E. *Individualism and Its Discontents: Appropriations of Emerson, 1880–1950*. Amherst: University of Massachusetts Press, 1997.

Olds, Jacqueline, and Richard S. Schwartz. *The Lonely American: Drifting Apart in the Twenty-First Century*. Boston: Beacon Press, 2009.

Russo, John Paul. "Loneliness and Solitude in Italian American Literature: Ciardi and Fante." In *American Solitudes: Proceedings of the Seventeenth Biennial International AISNA Conference*, 125–136. Rome: Carocci, 2007.

Slater, Philip. *The Pursuit of Loneliness: American Culture at the Breaking Point*. Boston: Beacon Press, 1970.

Storr, Anthony. *Solitude: A Return to the Self.* New York: Free Press, 1988.

Vermeule, Blakey. *Why Do We Care about Literary Characters?* Baltimore: Johns Hopkins University Press, 2010.

Warren, Robert Penn. "Why Do We Read Fiction?" In *New and Selected Essays*, 55–66. New York: Random House, 1989.

Weiss, Robert S. *Loneliness: The Experience of Emotional and Social Isolation.* Cambridge, MA: MIT Press, 1975.

Whicher, Stephen E. *Freedom and Fate: An Inner Life of Ralph Waldo Emerson.* New York: A. S. Barnes & Co., 1953.

——. *Selections from Ralph Waldo Emerson: An Organic Anthology.* Boston: Houghton Mifflin, 1957.

Wood, James. *How Fiction Works.* New York: Farrar, Straus and Giroux, 2008.

I. DOES NOBODY HERE KNOW RIP VAN WINKLE?

Primary Texts

Irving, Washington. *Diedrich Knickerbocker's "A History of New York"* [1809]. Edited by Stanley Williams and Tremaine McDowell. New York: Harcourt, Brace, 1927.

——. "Rip Van Winkle" [1819] from *The Sketch Book of Geofrey Crayon, Gent.,* edited by Haskell Springer. In *The Complete Works of Washington Irving,* edited by Richard Dilworth Rust, 8:28–42. Boston: Twayne, 1978.

——. *Salmagundi; or the Whimwhams and Opinions of Sir Launcelot Langstaff, Esq. & Others* [1807–1808]. Philadelphia: Lippincott, 1887.

Background Reading

Chudacoff, Howard P. *How Old Are You? Age Consciousness in American Culture.* Princeton, NJ: Princeton University Press, 1989.

Cole, Thomas R. *The Journey of Life: A Cultural History of Aging in America.* New York: Cambridge University Press, 1989.

Feibleman, James. *In Praise of Comedy: A Study in Its Theory and Practice.* New York: Macmillan, 1939.

Frost, Robert. *Complete Poems of Robert Frost.* New York: Holt, Rinehart, and Winston, 1964.

Hedges, William. *Washington Irving: An American Study, 1802–1832.* Baltimore: Johns Hopkins University Press, 1965.

Leary, Lewis. "The Two Voices of Washington Irving." In *From Irving to Steinbeck: Studies of American Literature in Honor of Harry Warfel,* edited by Motley Deakin and Peter Lisca, 13–26. Gainesville: University Press of Florida, 1972.

Linde, Charlotte. *Life Stories: The Creation of Coherence.* New York: Oxford University Press, 1993.

Rorabaugh, W. J. *The Alcoholic Republic: An American Tradition.* Oxford: Oxford University Press, 1979.

Rosenheim, Edward W., Jr. *Swift and the Satirist's Art.* Chicago: University of Chicago Press, 1963.

Rubin-Dorsky, Jeffrey. "Washington Irving and the Genesis of the Fiction Sketch." *Early American Literature* 21 (1986/87): 226–247.

Warner, Michael. "Irving's Posterity." *ELH* 67 (2000): 773–799.

Young, Philip. "Fallen from Time: The Mythic Rip Van Winkle." *Kenyon Review* 22 (1960): 547–573.

2. NATHANIEL HAWTHORNE DISSECTS BETRAYAL

Primary Texts

Hawthorne, Nathaniel. "Ethan Brand" [1851], and "My Kinsman, Major Molineux" [1832]. In *The Snow-Image and Uncollected Tales.* Vol. 11 of *The Centenary Edition of the Works of Nathaniel Hawthorne,* edited by Fredson Bowers, 83–102, 208–231. Columbus: Ohio State University Press, 1974.

——. *The House of the Seven Gables* [1851]. Vol. 2 in *The Centenary Edition of the Works of Nathaniel Hawthorne,* edited by Fredson Bowers. Columbus: Ohio State University Press, 1965.

Background Reading

Anderson, Quentin. *The Imperial Self: An Essay in American Literary and Cultural History.* New York: Alfred A. Knopf, 1971.

Baym, Nina. *The Shape of Hawthorne's Career.* Ithaca, NY: Cornell University Press, 1976.

Broes, Arthur T. "Journey into Moral Darkness: 'My Kinsman, Major Molineux' as Allegory." *Nineteenth-Century Fiction* 19 (September 1964): 171–184.

Carpenter, Richard C. "Hawthorne's Polar Explorations: 'Young Goodman Brown' and 'My Kinsman, Major Molineux.'" *Nineteenth-Century Fiction* 24 (June 1969): 45–56.

Colacurcio, Michael J. *The Province of Piety: Moral History in Hawthorne's Early Tales.* Cambridge, MA: Harvard University Press, 1984.

Gross, Seymour L., ed. *The House of the Seven Gables: An Authoritative Text, Backgrounds and Sources, Essays in Criticism.* Norton Critical Edition. New York: W. W. Norton, 1967.

Male, Roy R. *Hawthorne's Tragic Vision.* New York: W. W. Norton, 1957.

Mellow, James R. *Nathaniel Hawthorne in His Times.* Baltimore: Johns Hopkins University Press, 1980.

Miller, Edwin Haviland. *Salem Is My Dwelling Place: A Life of Nathaniel Hawthorne.* Iowa City: University of Iowa Press, 1991.

Miller, J. Hillis. *Hawthorne and History: Defacing It.* Cambridge, MA: Basil Blackwell, 1991.

Riesman, David. *The Lonely Crowd: A Study of the Changing American Character.* New Haven, CT: Yale University Press, 1950.

Rosenthal, Bernard, ed. *Critical Essays on Hawthorne's "The House of the Seven Gables."* New York: G. K. Hall, 1995.

Rouner, Leroy S., ed. *Loneliness.* Notre Dame, IN: University of Notre Dame Press, 1998.

Rozwenc, Edwin C. *The Compromise of 1850.* Boston: Heath, 1957.

Shklar, Judith N. "The Ambiguities of Betrayal." In Shklar, *Ordinary Vices,* 138–191. Cambridge, MA: Harvard University Press, 1984.

Swart, Koenread W. "'Individualism' in the Mid-Nineteenth Century (1826–1860)." *Journal of the History of Ideas* 23 (January–March 1962): 77–90.

Weaver, Richard M. "Two Types of American Individualism." *Modern Age: A Quarterly Review* 7 (Spring 1963): 119–134.

3. LOUISA MAY ALCOTT MEETS MARK TWAIN OVER THE YOUNG FACE OF CHANGE

Primary Texts

Alcott, Louisa May. *Little Women, or Meg, Jo, Beth, and Amy* [1868–1870]. Norton Critical Edition. Edited by Anne K. Phillips and Gregory Eiselein. New York: W. W. Norton, 2004.

———. *The Selected Letters of Louisa May Alcott.* Edited by Joel Myerson, Daniel Shealy, and Madeleine B. Stern. Boston: Little, Brown, 1987.

Twain, Mark. *Adventures of Huckleberry Finn* [1884–1885]. Berkeley and Los Angeles: University of California Press, 1985.

———. *The Adventures of Tom Sawyer* [1876]. New York: Oxford University Press, 1996.

Background Reading

Anderson, Quentin. *Making Americans: An Essay on Individualism and Money.* New York: Harcourt Brace Jovanovich, 1992.

Blair, Walter. *Mark Twain and Huck Finn.* Berkeley and Los Angeles: University of California Press, 1962.

Clausen, John S. "Adolescent Competence and the Shaping of the Life Course." *American Journal of Sociology* 96 (January 1991): 805–842.

Douglas, Ann. Introduction to *Little Women,* by Louisa May Alcott, xvii–xxvii. New York: Signet Classic, 1983.

Foote, Stephanie. "Resentful *Little Women:* Gender and Class Feeling in Louisa May Alcott." *College Literature* 32 (Winter 2005): 63–85.

Kaplan, Justin. *Mr. Clemens and Mark Twain: A Biography.* New York: Simon & Schuster, 1966.

Lerner, Laurence. *Angels and Absences: Child Deaths in the Nineteenth Century.* Nashville, TN: Vanderbilt University Press, 1997.

MacDonald, Ruth K. "Louisa May Alcott's *Little Women:* Who Is Still Reading Miss Alcott and Why." In *Touchstones: Reflections on the Best in Children's Literature,* vol. 1., edited by Perry Nodelman, 13–20. West Lafayette, IN: Children's Literature Association, 1985.

Mackey, Margaret. "*Little Women* Go to Market: Shifting Texts and Changing Readers." *Children's Literature in Education* 29 (1998): 153–173.

Matteson, John. *Eden's Outcasts: The Story of Louisa May Alcott and Her Father.* New York: W. W. Norton, 1997.

May, Jill P. "Feminism and Children's Literature: Fitting *Little Women* into the American Literary Canon." *CEA Critic: An Official Journal of the College English Association* 56 (Spring–Summer 1994): 19–27.

Moore, Timothy E., and Reet Mae. "Who Dies and Who Cries: Death and Bereavement in Children's Literature." *Journal of Communication (1986–1998)* 37 (Autumn 1987): 52–64.

Nelson, Claudia. "Family Circle or Vicious Circle? Anti-Paternal Undercurrents in Louisa May Alcott." In *The Child and the Family: Selected Papers from the 1988 International Conference of the Children's Literature Association*, 70–76. Pleasantville, NY: Pace University, 1988.

Sanchez-Eppler, Karen. *Dependent States: The Child's Part in Nineteenth-Century American Culture.* Chicago: University of Chicago Press, 2005.

Simpson, Claude M. *Twentieth Century Interpretations of "Adventures of Huckleberry Finn": A Collection of Critical Essays.* Englewood Cliffs, NJ: Prentice-Hall, 1968.

Smith, Henry Nash, ed. *Mark Twain: A Collection of Critical Essays.* Englewood Cliffs, NJ: Prentice-Hall, 1963.

Steinem, Gloria. *Revolution from Within: A Book of Self-Esteem.* Boston: Little, Brown, 1992.

4. HENRY JAMES AND ZORA NEALE HURSTON
ANSWER DEFEAT

Primary Texts

Hurston, Zora Neale. *Their Eyes Were Watching God* [1937]. Urbana and Chicago: University of Illinois Press, 1978.

James, Henry. *The Portrait of a Lady* [1881]. New York: Modern Library, 1944.

Background Reading

Barbeito, Patricia Felisa. "'Making Generations' in Jacobs, Larsen, and Hurston: A Genealogy of Black Women's Writing." *American Literature* 70 (June 1998): 365–395.

Buitenhuis, Peter, ed. *Twentieth Century Interpretations of "The Portrait of a Lady": A Collection of Critical Essays.* Englewood Cliffs, NJ: Prentice-Hall, 1968.

Davie, Sharon. "Free Mules, Talking Buzzards, and Cracked Plates: The Politics of Dislocation in *Their Eyes Were Watching God*." *PMLA* 108 (May 1993): 446–459.

Joseph, Philip. "The Verdict from the Porch: Zora Neale Hurston and Reparative Justice." *American Literature* 74 (September 2002): 455–483.

Kubitschek, Missy Dehn. "'Tuh De Horizon and Back': The Female Quest in *Their Eyes Were Watching God* and *Tar Baby*." *Callaloo* 13 (Summer 1990): 499–515.

Pippin, Robert B. *Henry James and Modern Life.* Cambridge: Cambridge University Press, 2000.

Silber, Ken. "An African-American Woman's Journey of Self-Discovery in Zora Neale Hurston's *Their Eyes Were Watching God*." In *Women in Literature: Reading through the Lens of Gender,* edited by Jerilyn Fisher. Westport, CT: Greenwood Press, 2003.

Spencer, Stephen. "The Value of Lived Experience: Zora Neale Hurston and the Complexity of Race." *Studies in American Culture* 27 (October 2004): 17–33.

Veeder, William. *Henry James—the Lessons of the Master: Popular Fiction and Personal Style in the Nineteenth Century.* Chicago: University of Chicago Press, 1975.

5. EDITH WHARTON'S ANATOMY OF BREAKDOWN

Primary Text

Wharton, Edith. *The Fruit of the Tree* [1907]. Boston: Northeastern University Press, 2000.

Background Reading

Bell, Millicent. Introduction to *The Cambridge Companion to Edith Wharton,* edited by Millicent Bell. Cambridge: Cambridge University Press, 1995.

——. *Edith Wharton and Henry James: The Story of Their Friendship.* New York: Braziller, 1965.

Campbell, Donna. Introduction to *The Fruit of the Tree*, by Edith Wharton, v–xli. Boston: Northeastern University Press, 2000.

Carlin, Deborah. "To Form a More Perfect Union: Gender, Tradition, and the Text in Wharton's *The Fruit of the Tree.*" In *Edith Wharton: New Critical Essays,* edited by Alfred Bendixen and Annette Zilversmit. New York: Garland, 1992.

Garden, Rebecca. "Sympathy, Disability, and the Nurse: Female Power in Edith Wharton's *The Fruit of the Tree.*" *Journal of Medical Humanities* (April 10, 2010). doi:10.1007/s10912-010-9115-3.

Goodman, Susan. *Edith Wharton's Women: Friends and Rivals.* Hanover, NH: University Press of New England, 1990.

Howe, Irving. "Introduction: The Achievement of Edith Wharton." In *Edith Wharton: A Collection of Critical Essays,* edited by Irving Howe. Englewood Cliffs, NJ: Prentice-Hall, 1962.

Lewis, R. W. B. *Edith Wharton: A Biography.* New York: Harper & Row, 1975.

Pascal, Blaise. *Pascal's Pensées.* Translated by Martin Turnell. London: Harvill Press, 1962.

Scarry, Elaine. *The Body in Pain: The Making and Unmaking of the World.* New York: Oxford University Press, 1985.

Shattuck, Roger. *Forbidden Knowledge: From Prometheus to Pornography.* New York: St. Martin's Press, 1996.

Tuttleton, James W. "Justine: Or, the Perils of Abstract Idealism." In *The Cambridge Companion to Edith Wharton,* edited by Millicent Bell. Cambridge: Cambridge University Press, 1995.

Wolff, Cynthia Griffin. *A Feast of Words: The Triumph of Edith Wharton.* New York: Oxford University Press, 1977.

MIDPOINT: THE LORDS OF LIFE REVISITED

Primary Text

Emerson, Ralph Waldo. "Experience." In *Essays: Second Series* [1844]. Vol. 3 of *The Collected Works of Ralph Waldo Emerson,* edited by Joseph Slater, Alfred R. Ferguson, and Jean Ferguson Carr, 25–49. Cambridge, MA: Belknap Press of Harvard University Press, 1983.

Background Reading

Buell, Lawrence. *Emerson.* Cambridge, MA: Harvard University Press, 2003.

Richardson, Robert D. *Emerson: The Mind on Fire; a Biography*. Berkeley and Los Angeles: University of California Press, 1995.

———. *First We Read, Then We Write: Emerson on the Creative Process.* Iowa City: University of Iowa Press, 2009.

Whicher, Stephen E. *Freedom and Fate: An Inner Life of Ralph Waldo Emerson.* Philadelphia: University of Pennsylvania Press, 1953.

———. *Selections from Ralph Waldo Emerson: An Organic Anthology.* Boston: Houghton Mifflin, 1957.

Windolph, Christopher J. *Emerson's Nonlinear Nature.* Columbia: University of Missouri Press, 2007.

6. THE IMMIGRANT NOVEL: FEAR IN AMERICA

Primary Text

Roth, Henry. *Call It Sleep* [1934]. New York: Farrar, Straus and Giroux, 2005.

Background Reading

Altenbernd, Lynn. "An American Messiah: Myth in Henry Roth's *Call It Sleep.*" *Modern Fiction Studies* 35 (Winter 1989): 673–687.

Diamant, Naomi. "Linguistic Universes in Henry Roth's *Call It Sleep.*" *Contemporary Literature* 27 (Autumn 1986): 336–355.

Ferguson, James. "Symbolic Patterns in *Call It Sleep.*" *Twentieth Century Literature* 14 (January 1969): 211–220.

Ferraro, Thomas J. *Ethnic Passages: Literary Immigrants in Twentieth-Century America.* Chicago: University of Chicago Press, 1993.

Guttman, Allen. *The Jewish Writer in America: Assimilation and the Crisis of Identity.* New York: Oxford University Press, 1971.

Kazin, Alfred. "The Art of 'Call It Sleep.'" *New York Review of Books,* October 10, 1991, 15–18.

Ledbetter, Kenneth. "Henry Roth's *Call It Sleep:* The Revival of a Proletarian Novel." *Twentieth Century Literature* 12 (October 1966): 123–130.

Lesser, Wayne. "A Narrative's Revolutionary Energy: The Example of Henry Roth's *Call It Sleep.*" *Criticism* 23 (Spring 1981): 155–176.

Sollors, Werner. *Consent and Descent in American Culture.* New York: Oxford University Press, 1986.

Wirth-Nesher, Hana, ed. *New Essays on "Call It Sleep."* Cambridge: Cambridge University Press, 1996.

7. WILLIAM FAULKNER AND TONI MORRISON
PLOT RACIAL DIFFERENCE

Primary Texts

Faulkner, William. *Absalom, Absalom!* [1936]. New York: Random House, 1964.

Morrison, Toni. *Beloved.* New York: Random House, 1987.

——. *Playing in the Dark: Whiteness and the Literary Imagination.* Cambridge, MA: Harvard University Press, 1992.

——. "The Site of Memory." In *Inventing the Truth: The Art and Craft of Memoir,* edited by William Zinsser, 83–102. Boston: Houghton Mifflin, 1995.

Background Reading

Adler, Alfred. "Psychiatric Aspects Regarding Individual and Social Disorganization." *American Journal of Sociology* 42 (May 1937): 773–780.

Bloom, Harold, ed. *Toni Morrison: Modern Critical Views.* New York: Chelsea House, 1990.

Carden, Mary Paniccia. "Models of Memory and Romance: The Dual Endings of Toni Morrison's *Beloved*." *Twentieth Century Literature* 45 (Winter 1999): 401–427.

Cheng, Ann Anlin. *The Melancholy of Race: Psychoanalysis, Assimilation, and Hidden Grief.* New York: Oxford University Press, 2001.

Davis, Kimberly Chabot. "'Postmodern Blackness': Toni Morrison's *Beloved* and the End of History." *Twentieth Century Literature* (Summer 1998): 242–290.

Hareven, Tamara K. "The History of the Family and the Complexity of Social Change." *American Historical Review* 96 (February 1991): 95–124.

Heller, Dana. "Reconstructing Kin: Family, History, and Narrative in Toni Morrison's *Beloved*." *College Literature* 21 (June 1994): 105–117.

Herlihy, David. "Family." *American Historical Review* 96 (February 1991): 1–16.

Hobson, Fred, ed. *William Faulkner's "Absalom, Absalom!" A Casebook.* New York: Oxford University Press, 2003.

Kinney, Arthur F., ed. *Critical Essays on William Faulkner: The Sutpen Family.* New York: G. K. Hall, 1996.

Muhlenfeld, Elisabeth. *William Faulkner's "Absalom, Absalom!": A Critical Study.* New York: Garland, 1984.

Ragan, David Paul. *William Faulkner's "Absalom, Absalom!": A Critical Study.* Ann Arbor, MI: UMI Research Press, 1987.

Taylor-Guthrie, Danielle. *Conversations with Toni Morrison.* Jackson: University Press of Mississippi, 1994.

8. SAUL BELLOW OBSERVES OLD AGE

Primary Text

Bellow, Saul. *Mr. Sammler's Planet, A Novel.* New York: Viking Press, 1969.

Background Reading

Austin, Mike. "The Genesis of the Speaking Subject in *Mr. Sammler's Planet.*" *Saul Bellow Journal* 10, no. 2 (1992): 25–36.

Birnbaum, Milton. "The Aging Process: A Literary Perspective." *World and I* 3 (March 1995): 426–439.

Corner, Martin. "Moving Outwards: Consciousness, Discourse, and Attention in Saul Bellow's Fiction." *Studies in the Novel* 32 (Fall 2000): 369–385.

Galloway, David. "*Mr. Sammler's Planet:* Bellow's Failure of Nerve." *Modern Fiction Studies* 19 (Spring 1973): 17–28.

Gove, Walter R., Suzanne T. Ortega, and Carolyn Briggs Style. "The Maturational and Role Perspectives on Aging and Self through the Adult Years." *American Journal of Sociology* 94 (March 1989): 1117–1145.

Guttmann, Allen. "Saul Bellow's Mr. Sammler." *Contemporary Literature* 14 (Spring 1973): 157–168.

Hoggatt, Douglas. "Reconciliation and the Natural Knowledge of the Soul in *Mr. Sammler's Planet.*" *Saul Bellow Journal* 13, no. 1 (1995): 3–21.

Neugarten, Bernice. "Age Groups in American Society and the Rise of the Young-Old." *Annals of the American Academy of Political and Social Science* 415 (1974): 187–198.

Parini, Jay. "Mr. Sammler, Hero of Our Time." *Salmagundi* (Spring 1995): 66–70.

Posner, Richard A. *Aging and Old Age.* Chicago: University of Chicago Press, 1995.

Wright, Derek. "The Mind's Blind Eye: Saul Bellow's *Mr. Sammler's Planet.*" *International Fiction Review* 22, nos. 1 & 2 (1995): 21–24.

9. DON DELILLO AND MARILYNNE ROBINSON MOURN LOSS

Primary Texts

DeLillo, Don. *Falling Man.* New York: Scribner, 2007.

——. "In the Ruins of the Future: Reflections on Terror and Loss in the Shadow of September." *Harper's Magazine,* December 2001, 33–40.

Junod, Tom. "The Falling Man." *Esquire,* September 2003, 177–181.

Robinson, Marilynne. *Gilead.* New York: Farrar, Straus and Giroux, 2004.

Background Reading

Acocella, Joan. "A Note of the Miraculous." *New York Review of Books,* June 9, 2005.

Besser, Carin. "A Writer's Time: An Interview with Marilynne Robinson." *New Yorker,* September 13, 2004.

Churchill, Larry R. "The Human Experience of Dying: The Moral Primacy of Stories over Stages." *Soundings* 62 (Spring 1979): 24–37.

Grief, Mark. "Alzheimer's America." *London Review of Books,* July 5, 2007, 19–20.

Hadley, Tessa. "An Attic Full of Sermons." *London Review of Books,* April 21, 2005, 19–20.

Junod, Tom. "The Man Who Invented 9/11." *Esquire,* June 2007, 38–39.

Kakutani, Michiko. "A Man, a Woman and a Day of Terror." *New York Times,* May 9, 2007, E1.

Kauffman, Linda S. "The Wake of Terror: Don DeLillo's 'In The Ruins of the Future,' 'Baader-Meinhof,' and *Falling Man.*" *Modern Fiction Studies* 54, no. 2 (Summer 2008): 353–377.

LeClair, Thomas, and Don DeLillo. "An Interview with Don DeLillo." *Contemporary Literature* 23 (Winter 1982): 19–31.

Leonard, John. "New Books." *Harper's Magazine,* December 2004, 87–88.

McClure, John A. "Postmodern/Post-Secular: Contemporary Fiction and Spirituality." *Modern Fiction Studies* 41, no. 1 (Spring 1995): 141–163.

Mensch, Betty. "Review: Jonathan Edwards, *Gilead,* and the Problem of 'Tradition.'" *Journal of Law and Religion* 21 (2005/2006): 221–241.

Miner, Valerie. "Iowa Meditations." *Women's Review of Books,* December 2004, 19.

Osteen, Mark. *American Magic and Dread: Don DeLillo's Dialogue with Culture.* Philadelphia: University of Pennsylvania Press, 2000.

Rich, Frank. "The Clear Blue Sky." *New York Times,* May 27, 2007, sec. 7, p. 1.

Shy, Todd. "Religion and Marilynne Robinson." *Salmagundi* 155/156 (Summer 2007): 251–264.

Szalai, Jennifer. "After the Fall: Don DeLillo without His Towers." *Harper's Magazine,* July 2007, 91–96.

Tanner, Laura A. "'Looking Back from the Grave': Sensory Perception and the Anticipation of Absence in Marilynne Robinson's *Gilead.*" *Contemporary Literature* 48, no. 2 (Summer 2007): 227–252.

Versluys, Kristiann. *Out of the Blue: September 11 and the Novel.* New York: Columbia University Press, 2009.

Wood, James. "The Homecoming: A Prodigal Son Returns in Marilynne Robinson's Third Novel." *New Yorker,* September 8, 2008, 76–77.

10. WALT WHITMAN FINDS THE COURAGE TO BE

Primary Texts

Cicero. "In Defence of the Poet Aulus Licinius Archias" [62 BC]. In *Selected Political Speeches of Cicero,* edited by Michael Grant, 146–164. New York: Penguin, 1969.

Tillich, Paul. *The Courage to Be.* New Haven, CT: Yale University Press, 1952.

Whitman, Walt. *Specimen Days* [1882]. In *Walt Whitman: Complete Poetry and Collected Prose,* edited by Justin Kaplan, 675–926. New York: Library of America, 1982.

Background Reading

Aarnes, William. "'Cut This Out': Whitman Liberating the Reader in *Specimen Days.*" *Walt Whitman Review* 27 (March 1981): 25–32.

——. "'Free Margins': Identity and Silence in Whitman's *Specimen Days.*" *ESQ: A Journal of the American Renaissance* 28 (4th Quarter 1982): 243–260.

——. "Withdrawal and Resumption: Whitman and Society in the Last Two Parts of *Specimen Days.*" In *Studies in the American Renaissance, 1982,* edited by Joel Myerson, 401–432. Boston: Twayne Publishers, 1982.

Balkun, Mary McAleer. "Whitman's *Specimen Days* and the Culture of Authenticity." *Walt Whitman Quarterly* 17 (Summer–Fall 1999): 15–24.

Cumming, Mark. "Carlyle, Whitman, and the Disimprisonment of Epic." *Victorian Studies* 22 (Winter 1986): 207–226.

Friedman, Rohn S. "A Whitman Primer: Solipsism and Identity." *American Quarterly* 27 (October 1985): 443–460.

Hutchinson, George B. "Life Review and the Common World in Whitman's *Specimen Days*." *South Atlantic Review* 52 (November 1987): 3–23.

Kaplan, Justin. *Walt Whitman: A Life.* New York: Simon & Schuster, 1980.

Kuusisto, Stephen. "Walt Whitman's 'Specimen Days' and the Discovery of the Disability Memoir." *Prose Studies* 27 (April–August 2005): 155–162.

Miller, James E., Jr. *Walt Whitman.* New Haven, CT: College and University Press, 1962.

Mishra, Rabi Shankar. "*Specimen Days:* 'An Immensely Negative Book.'" *Delta* 16 (May 1983): 95–110.

Mullin, John Eugene. "The Whitman of *Specimen Days*." *Iowa Review* 24 (Winter 1994): 148–161.

Philippon, Daniel J. "'I Only Seek to Put You in Rapport': Message and Method in Walt Whitman's *Specimen Days*." In *Reading the Earth: New Directions in the Study of Literature and Environment,* edited by Michael P. Branch, Rochelle Johnson, Daniel Patterson, and Scott Slovic, 179–193. Moscow: University of Idaho Press, 1998.

Price, Kenneth. "Whitman on Other Writers: Controlled 'Graciousness' in *Specimen Days*." *ESQ: A Journal of the American Renaissance* 26 (2nd Quarter 1980): 79–87.

Scholnick, Robert J. "'How Dare a Sick Man or an Obedient Man Write Poems?': Whitman and the Dis-ease of the Perfect Body." In *Disability Studies: Enabling the Humanities,* edited by Sharon L. Snyder, Brenda Jo Brueggemann, and Rosemarie Garland-Thomson, 248–259. New York: Modern Language Association of America, 2002.

Sennett, Richard. *The Craftsman.* New Haven, CT: Yale University Press, 2008.

Zweig, Paul. *Walt Whitman: The Making of the Poet.* New York: Basic Books, 1984.

INDEX